Successful Practising

A handbook for pupils, parents and music teachers

Jenny Macmillan

ISBN 978-0-9566189-0-0

Published by
Jenny Macmillan
17 Lynfield Lane
Cambridge
CB4 1DR
UK

Cover design by
DragonArtz

Contents

Cum gaudio quaerens

Seeking with joy

Writings of Dogen (1200-1253)

Acknowledgements

This book has been incubating for many years, but the eventual motivation to write it came from a long, unpublished article by the violin teacher Jean Hickson. As soon as I saw this article I knew it contained many good ideas which should become more widely known. Jean kindly allowed me to use her ideas in my book in whatever way I wished.

Other inspiration has come from attending conferences and masterclasses, observing lessons, and discussing the subject with colleagues. I particularly valued playing in masterclasses with Murray McLachlan on two music courses in the Lot Valley in France. These gave me the opportunity to observe his insightful teaching at first hand and to discuss matters of practice at length (see his two comprehensive articles, *The Practice List*[1]).

I received invaluable help from several colleagues and friends – teachers and parents, musicians and non-musicians – who spent hours reading the manuscript at various stages and articulating their views. I would especially like to thank Rodney Slatford, Heli Ignatius-Fleet, Jimmy Altham, Graham Garrett, Lilian Hall, Sheila Webster, Wendy and Mike Addison, and Margaret Neill; and Polly Waterfield who also helpfully wrote the suggestions for practising a Brahms Waltz on the violin. I would like to acknowledge the help given by the late Miffy McFarlane.

I would like to credit my tutor for my master's course in Psychology for Musicians at Sheffield University, Stephanie Pitts, who showed me how to study existing research material, how to conduct my own research, and how to organise a vast quantity of material and condense it into an essay, an article or a dissertation. In this I have been helped enormously, too, by my husband, Sebastian, who has been, in effect, my editor-in-chief as well as my mainstay in assisting with computer issues. His patience and his willingness to share his knowledge seem boundless. Thanks to our son, Nick, for his help with the diagrams and front cover, and to our daughter, Pippa, for help with the musical examples.

Finally, I would like to thank my own music teachers and my piano pupils who have been the vital inspiration for this book. Without the experience of working with these teachers and pupils, this book would not exist. Although supported by research into the music teaching literature, this book is based firmly on my experiences as a student and as a teacher, and also as a parent. As such, I hope it will help other students, teachers and parents.

Jenny Macmillan

Biographical note

I am a Suzuki piano teacher and teacher trainer with a thriving practice in Cambridge of pupils aged from three to 18. I give lecture/demonstrations throughout the UK. My three children studied piano to a high level. The youngest, Pippa, is a professional double bass player who also runs her own flourishing cello and double bass teaching practice. My many published articles appear on my website: www.jennymacmillan.co.uk.

Foreword

It goes without saying that in order to develop as a musician you need to practise hard. It is, therefore, surprising to report how often ignorance, helplessness and even despair are encountered when discussing this subject with music students. This is because practice really is an art in itself, a solitary vocation, and it takes considerable self-will, understanding and experience to learn how to cope with it. Of course, many children are lucky enough to have parents who are willing to supervise their practice, but even here there are pitfalls. Supervisors can make the fatal mistake of assuming that 'spoon feeding' and endless mechanical drilling is the same thing as productive practice. Drilling without listening will not free the artistic spirit, and solving young students' problems for them will lead only to perpetual dependency and, ultimately, to boredom and rebellion away from music.

Whilst it is good to think that all reputable teachers will help their students in methodology of practice, providing the requisite guidance, it is nonetheless fair to say that this is usually not enough. Developing musicians take literally years and years to cultivate good practising techniques, which should always be inspired, creative and, to quote Claudio Arrau, who practised vociferously, "beautiful". This is where Jenny's concentrated, practical and extremely organised book comes into its own. By systematically listing and describing a veritable practiser's universe, pupils and their supervising parents have sensible and inspiring advice at their fingertips. The book is so much more than the sum of its parts in that the ideas and approaches it outlines can be taken away, studied and applied, then thought through in terms of the broad picture. I know you will find it as illuminating, down-to-earth and comprehensively essential as I have done.

Murray McLachlan

How to use this book

Ideally, I would recommend first quickly reading through the whole of the book to get an idea of what it covers.

Next, or for those who have little time to do that, I would recommend turning to **Section Two: How to practise**, especially **Chapter 4: Practice strategies**, **Chapter 5: Practising specific issues** and **Chapter 6: Learning new pieces**, and glancing speedily over it. Pianists and other keyboard players could also look at **Chapter 7: Practising for pianists**.

It would be perfectly possible to pick one practice strategy at random, eg *Practise the passage staccato as well as legato* or *Memorise awkward page turns* or *Every day practise a short section (eg a page, or two lines) very slowly*, and apply it to one or every piece/study/scale you are currently learning.

Another, perhaps better, way would be to look at one of your pieces, decide what you would like to improve in it (eg accuracy, fluency, ornaments) and find several strategies to address that issue. You will prefer some ways to others; some will be more effective in that particular place than others. So experiment with several strategies and repeatedly use those that work best for you in that piece.

Adapt strategies to suit your purpose. Combine two or more. When you find one you like, apply it to other parts of the same piece, and to other pieces. Apply it regularly, at every day's practice, so you gradually develop and master that skill.

Enjoy the challenge to improve your playing!

Introduction

Making music is stimulating, exciting, challenging and enjoyable. It may also be relaxing and therapeutic. Children and adults alike may find it restful to sit and play pieces, or to improvise, after a day at school or at work. Sight reading duets with a friend or playing in a small ensemble such as a string quartet is fun, as well as providing the basis for social interaction. Singing in a choir or playing in a band or orchestra offers yet other delights, rehearsals often leading to the thrill of a performance. Music is an art, through which one can gain a broader view of life.

Central to developing musical skill on an instrument is efficient and effective practice. Practice is essential in order to develop technical and musical skills, to learn and memorise music, and to prepare for performance. There are two key issues regarding practice – one is quantity and the other is quality. Unless the student practises regularly for a reasonable length of time, progress will be poor. But even if a student does put in the hours, progress is unlikely to be good unless the practice is focused. Practice needs to be an informed, rather than a hit-and-miss, affair.

What would be a student's reaction if asked to record a practice for their teacher to listen to? The chances are they would react with horror at the thought of recording a home practice. And this says it all! Practising is a skill. It needs to be learned. It needs to be taught. Students should be proud of the way they practise, of their ability to practise. But many are ashamed or embarrassed. They don't really know what they should be doing. As Paul Harris says, "If only all pupils could learn to make *some* decent use of all that time between lessons, what an effect it might have on their rate of progress"[2]. Anders Ericsson refers to "deliberate practice"[3]. Daniel Coyle calls it "deep practice"[4]. They all mean thoughtful practice, paying attention to technique and sound, judging critically and focusing on improving weaknesses. However, instrumental teachers are rarely trained to teach students how to practise.

Parents, particularly of primary aged children, are increasingly becoming more involved in their children's schooling by helping with reading and maths. Many parents say they would like to help with music practice but feel they do not know how. There seems to be no readily accessible book of ideas that a teacher can give to pupils and parents to study. *Successful Practising* aims to demystify the process of practice, to collate some of the more useful research findings, and to provide some ideas that may be helpful.

As well as assisting parents to support their young children in their musical studies, *Successful Practising* aims to enable older, more independent music students to make the best use of their practice time, so it is not a daily chore but rather a source of inspiration and satisfaction. The first section of this book encourages families and teachers to create a positive learning environment for children. The second section of the book is directed mainly towards teenagers and adult students who are practising independently, although its ideas on how to practise are applicable also to parents and young children. Teachers may find many ideas to pass on to their pupils to benefit their practice and, therefore, their progress.

What is practice?

It is important to differentiate between *practising* an instrument and *playing* it. Playing an instrument means playing through a piece or improvising for instant enjoyment or emotional satisfaction and there is, of course, a place for these activities. But we need to practise in order to improve. Practising is purposeful work which develops the skills that form the link between the musical intention and its execution. Practising implies working on a short section, listening carefully to the tone quality, intonation, rhythm, articulation, breathing, phrasing, dynamics, and so on, and being aware of the physical movements involved. Students need to be clear *what* they are to practise, *how* they are to practise it, and *why*.

Learning an instrument is really about learning to understand and master principles. The principles of good performance remain similar whatever the level; so do the principles of good practice. Musical performance requires beautiful tone, good intonation, clear rhythms, precise articulation, careful breathing, accurate dynamics, musical phrasing and natural posture, in order to communicate a meaningful artistic experience to the audience (even an audience of only one – the performer). Good practising involves identifying problems, devising strategies to overcome the difficulties, and repeating short sections while listening carefully for musical sounds. These elements develop in subtlety as students mature, but essentially remain the same from age three to adult, from learning and performing folk songs to concertos.

In the long term, serious focused practice is much more satisfying than spending practice time simply playing though one's pieces. But in the short term real practising, which engages both the emotions and the intellect, can be hard work. Once students find through experience that thoughtful, planned practice enables them to make progress, the whole concept of practice becomes much more manageable and enjoyable. Practice now becomes challenging in both senses of the word – difficult, yes, but also offering a sense of focus, interest, achievement and pleasure.

Anyone not making good progress at their musical instrument should consider carefully how they are practising. Is the practice efficient, or is much time being wasted? Are the points discussed in the lesson really repeated in practice, or are they just thought about, or ignored, and then the piece played through? Playing through a piece with mistakes may be worse than not practising it at all – the student is just repeating errors and learning better how to perform the mistakes. However, if practising is thorough, skills can be developed so that what was difficult becomes easy. In this way the student builds a library of musical and technical skills which are transferred from one piece of music to the next. Often, if the student plays more than one instrument, musical skills, or principles, will be transferred from one instrument to another. Not only that, but successful working habits, learned through music practice, will be transferred to other areas of life.

In her unpublished article, Jean Hickson described music practice as:

- ❑ independent learning between lessons

- ❑ something that children often don't like doing, but most teachers and parents expect!

- ❑ focused work in order to build the technique that makes the playing more fun

- ❑ something that needs to be taught and monitored over many years by teachers and parents

- ❑ something that must eventually be done for oneself[5].

Elsewhere it has been identifed as:

❏ that which achieves the desired end product, in as short a time as possible, without interfering with long-term goals[6].

These are carefully considered adult accounts compared with rather more prosaic ideas from children, reported in Jean Hickson's article as:

❏ repetitive stuff and boring

❏ working on difficult bits

❏ what you have to do to play well

❏ a chore that has to be done to 'get good'

❏ not much fun

❏ not as enjoyable as playing.

So the question is how to reconcile these two viewpoints and how to persuade pupils to see things from their parents' and teachers' angle. How can practice become an enjoyable and productive session each day?

Of those who have ever played a musical instrument, there can be few who have not, at some time or another, had a confrontation about practice. The word has emotive connotations: family members disagree about its time, place, detail and even existence; parents and their offspring argue about it; pupils who are otherwise reasonable and honest human beings tell terrible untruths to their teachers about it.

All would-be instrumentalists know that they must practice. Most have a fair idea of the ideal frequency and duration of this practice and it is almost always more than they do. For most of us, this can induce feelings of guilt and negativity, inhibiting the next potential practice and locking us into a negative circle, instead of the ideal positive circle of:

This is, of course, simplistic, but nevertheless is perhaps not given the consideration that it is due. So we need ways of making practice sessions productive and enjoyable. A little like a good diet, perhaps, if it contains some tasty and yet nutritious items it is more likely that we will stick to it.

Why practise?

Learners of any skill need to practise that skill in order to become experts or even reasonable exponents. This applies right across the board, to all sports (eg golf, tennis, football, horse-riding), many games (chess and bridge come to mind), and many practical skills (such as typing, sewing and woodwork). Most skills involve many integral parts – different manoeuvres, movements, co-ordinations, judgements – some of which are more complex than others. Playing a musical instrument, arguably, involves some of the most complex skills. Alongside learning to play in a musical, expressive and communicative way, basic techniques must be mastered. Reading music – translating the composer's dots and dashes into melody and rhythm – is another complex task to be acquired by the would-be musician.

Technical difficulties will be encountered early on. Small inexperienced fingers find it hard to locate the correct place on a given string and stay there, bows refuse to do as their operator wishes, lips very quickly get tired trying to play woodwind and brass instruments, and the co-ordination of two hands on a keyboard (and, for older students, two hands and two feet on an organ) may seem almost impossible.

In the early stages of learning, much practice time needs to be directed towards minimising the difficulties of that particular instrument, and making some of the more basic movements begin to become automatic. This is where repetition comes in – basic exercises need to be repeated many times. Repetitions can be made fun by, for example, rolling a dice for the number to be performed each day. This is also where the strategic use of charts, stars, or some other method of registering repetitions can be invaluable.

Here are some illuminating comments from pupils who increased their practice time for a two-week period when participating in a sponsored practice for ill children:

- ❏ It's been an incentive to do better at each practice.
- ❏ Good practice makes you feel confident, then you do better practice.
- ❏ I felt a real sense of achievement.
- ❏ After two weeks of good practice I feel a rhythm and flow to the violin.
- ❏ The sponsored practice really helped me to get a routine going.
- ❏ Thinking about sick children made me practise harder[5].

And from a parent:

- ❏ As a parent, I can now clearly see the difference practice makes[5].

And some words of wisdom from professional musicians and researchers:

- ❏ There are no short cuts to achieving your goals in music – practice is the only way[7].
- ❏ Half an hour playing with awareness is worth six hours without it[8].
- ❏ Muscle memories are much harder to lay down than mind memories – they take practice, practice, practice. But once ingrained, they are far more difficult to erase[9].
- ❏ High achievers practise the most, moderate achievers practise a moderate amount, and low achievers practise hardly at all[10].

Successful practising

There is no magic trick for progress on a musical instrument. The one certain distinguishing feature of successful musicians at whatever level is that, at some stage in their lives, they have practised, and practised conscientiously. Remember the only time success comes before work is in the dictionary. Success comes much more readily when skill development is conducted in the most efficient way.

Musicians practise to become technically proficient, to learn and memorise repertoire, to develop musical interpretations, and to prepare for performance. The fundamental but complex skills required to play a piece of music need to become automatic in order to allow the brain to concentrate on the higher musical aspects of interpretation. Compare this with driving a car where, with practice, the basics of steering, braking and gear-changing become automatic responses, allowing the experienced driver to concentrate on reacting to the road and traffic conditions.

Section One

Creating a learning environment

Section One: Creating a learning environment

The road to becoming an accomplished musician is challenging and exciting, though long and complex. Parents can help right from the beginning by creating a comfortable learning environment – supplying the necessary equipment as well as creating a positive atmosphere. A suitable instrument is essential, preferably in a warm, light, quiet room, away from the distractions of family, friends, telephone, television, DVD player and computer. An appropriate stool or chair is necessary, together with a music stand (unless the child is learning the piano), and also sheet music. A collection of recordings is extremely helpful (see **Listening to music** on page 34).

Just as important as this essential equipment is a positive, encouraging atmosphere. Parents may sing to and with their young children. They may listen to classical music on CDs, the internet and the radio, take their youngsters to children's concerts, and enthuse about music. Parents can help by planning the schedule for each day, ensuring there is space for music practice between school, meals, homework, socialising, hobbies and other activities. Children may need to be taken to their music lessons. Parents could consider the benefit to their child of themselves attending the instrumental lessons (with the agreement of the teacher) and taking notes on ways of helping their child at home. They may also consider assisting their child with practice. It is very supportive if both parents attend pupils' concerts.

Musical children are formed by:

- ❑ praise – lots of it
- ❑ discipline – kind but firm
- ❑ step-by-step learning – mastering small musical and technical steps
- ❑ achievement – accompanied by appropriate praise and congratulations
- ❑ fine music – listening to plenty of high quality performances.

The ultimate aim is to enable pupils to become independent. Instilling good learning habits is an excellent start.

To involve parents or not?

The question of whether parents should be involved when children learn a musical instrument is a contentious one. There are many teachers who do not involve parents in the learning process, and who have good reasons for their views. Other teachers allow parents to get involved, or even encourage active parental participation in lessons and/or practices (see boxes on the next three pages).

Numerous research studies have reported that parental involvement in general education improves student achievement[11]. Studies of reading skills have argued that parental involvement – reading to their children, having books in the home, and hearing their children read – is vital for reading attainment[12]. Studies involving children at all levels, from infancy to secondary school, show that parental involvement makes a difference, even that parents are critical to children's successes during the school years[13].

Almost all parents are interested in their children's education[14]. However, many are unaware of the real improvement that even a relatively small effort on their part may bring about. They are conscious of their own limitations as teachers, and feel they do not know what to do, or how, in order to give effective help and encouragement. The most important qualities required are sensitivity, patience, enthusiasm, common sense and perseverance, rather than particular instructional skills or teaching techniques. Parents who doubt their ability to help their children learn, commit their children's education entirely to teachers; parents who are confident, guide their children's learning and participate actively in the life of the school.

Attitudes to parental involvement

In my own research, teachers, parents and pupils were interviewed to ascertain their attitudes towards parental involvement when children learn a musical instrument[15]. I found that teachers were equally divided in their views on parental involvement in children's music lessons and practices (see table on next page). Teachers who discourage parental involvement put forward many convincing arguments. They say that parents tend to interfere, parents inhibit the development of an independent pupil-teacher relationship, teachers want children to be independent in their practice, and parental over-involvement may be discouraging or confusing. Conversely, other teachers give good reasons for encouraging parental involvement. They say that it is beneficial for parents to see in the context of a lesson their children's achievements, challenges, problems and goals, that practice is more efficient when supervised and that it is best to explain it directly to the parent. They also emphasise the enjoyment of parent and child making music together. Teachers who encourage parental assistance with practice consider it particularly useful in the early stages of learning an instrument, for younger pupils, and when preparing for examinations.

In my sample, the teachers' promotion of parental involvement was very varied. At the end of lessons, some teachers discuss the lesson. Some teachers invite parents to follow the lesson with a view to helping with practice, or they draw the parent's attention to good achievements. Other teachers are not specific about what parents should do, and the parents sit at the other end of the room and either read or listen to the lesson.

It is rare for teachers to instruct parents in how to supervise their children's practice on a moment-by-moment basis. Some teachers ask parents to encourage practice to take place, help if the child asks, read the child's practice notes, act as an appreciative audience, and engage in ensemble playing with the child.

Parents say they may encourage practice to take place, ensure everything gets practised, instruct their child, engage in ensemble playing, listen when asked, or encourage their child. Several parents say they would like to make music with their child but consider they are not good enough. However, many musically untrained parents are willing and able to assist their children with practice.

It is evident that parents are more able to act as an intermediary between the teacher and the child than teachers realise. It is not necessary for parents to be musically trained to help their children. Crucially, I found that children who receive parental help, welcome it.

A key issue seems to be encouraging parents to help in a positive, non-critical way. To be successfully involved, it is necessary that parents have confidence in their own potential to contribute.

Studies have shown that the amount of time spent by parents in supervising music practice is a better predictor of student achievement in the early stages of development than the total amount of time spent practising[10]. It does seem that supervised practice can create excellent conditions for focused practice, resulting in improved skill development.

Advantages and disadvantages of parental involvement[15]

Advantages for the child
- ❑ More progress and achievement – increased discipline increases quality of practice which increases effectiveness of practice
- ❑ More efficient – saves time if parent can guide practice
- ❑ More effective – parent can help child practise correctly and consistently
- ❑ Playing music together is more fun
- ❑ Personal and social development – enriches child's life, raises self-esteem, opportunity to succeed in front of parent, special time with parent – reassuring, motivating and encouraging

Disadvantages for the child
- ❑ Lack of independence – prevents free-thinking of child – difficult for child to take responsibility for own practice
- ❑ Parental interference or over-involvement may be discouraging
- ❑ Pressure of overbearing parent, or one whose expectations are too high – fear of failure or disapproval
- ❑ Issues of authority – confusion can arise
- ❑ Relationship between parent and teacher could hinder child's progress
- ❑ Issue of when parent should disengage and let child become independent

Advantages for the parent
- ❑ Enjoyable and satisfying to be part of child's learning process, to gain insight into how child learns and to see child's achievements, challenges, problems and goals
- ❑ Parent may learn from teacher about positive language and views when working with child
- ❑ May improve parent/child relationship

Disadvantages for the parent
- ❑ Stressful
- ❑ Time-consuming
- ❑ Boring
- ❑ Problem of managing siblings
- ❑ Other parent could feel excluded
- ❑ Expectations could be too high
- ❑ Could damage parent/child relationship

Advantages for the teacher	Disadvantages for the teacher
❏ Saves time – parent can take notes during lesson	❏ Attendance inhibits intimacy of independent pupil-teacher relationship
❏ More progress – parent can help with practice and can interpret teacher's comments	❏ Parent may interfere during lesson
	❏ Teacher may not wish to be observed
❏ Quality, quantity and consistency of practice leads to satisfaction of seeing good progress	❏ More preparation required
	❏ Difficult to manage parent expectations with ambitious parents
❏ Enjoyable to relate to more members of pupil's family – trusting relationship and friendship	❏ Parent may undermine teacher's authority
❏ Important insight into home situation	❏ May be issues of musical interpretation and technique if parent is musically experienced

Most of the disadvantages can be avoided if parents are encouraged to become involved in the right way.

Chapter 1: Parents

Support and encouragement

The greatest gifts that parents of aspiring musicians can give to their children are support and encouragement. This need not necessarily mean being around at every practice time, for the child needs to experience practising alone, but it does mean ensuring, as far as possible, that the whole musical experience is a good one – and that includes practice! It means taking the trouble to find out what is needed and expected and facilitating the whole process.

Children need to believe that they can learn to play, provided they have a real desire to do so. They need to know how to practise and they need to see that good practice leads to progress and progress leads to increasing pleasure. Success and achievement will help build their confidence and self-esteem. The relationship between work done and pleasure and satisfaction eventually derived should be emphasised. Effort and results should be honestly assessed, and parents should feel free to reward both.

Music in the home

As far as possible, make practice the norm rather than an optional extra. One of the reasons why musicians tend to beget musicians is that music is seen as normal in that household. It is the same with sport and reading and many other activities – children tend to be absorbed into their home culture. When there is music around – instruments, recordings providing a variety of musical styles, people practising and making music together – it is an easier and more natural learning situation for the child.

Ideally, the family of an aspiring young musician will invite other musicians to come to their house to play live music. This could involve inviting another pupil, of a similar age to your child, of the same teacher. Each child plays one or two pieces to the two families in an informal 'concert', followed by a tea party. Children growing up in such an environment have advantages over those without this background. Nevertheless, these fortunate children are not the only ones to succeed. The single most important distinguishing factor is practice – how much, how effective, and how high the motivation to work through all the challenges presented.

Even if music is not really the norm, parents can help with a timetable that allows easy access to a practice slot. Practice needs to be given a reasonably high profile – to be important, and to figure as an activity to be respected – but at the same time, it should be kept in perspective and not afforded importance that is way above what is reasonable. It is seldom the be-all-and-end-all of existence. A strict routine for practice is not always entirely necessary. There are many varied ways of organising practice. But certainly in the early stages, routine helps in that at least practice gets done as opposed to not done! Without practice, progress will be minimal and, necessarily, very slow.

Getting started

Often it is not the actual practice that is the problem for so many youngsters, but rather the decision to do it. We human beings can be terrible procrastinators. One effective strategy is to plan at the end of one practice what you will do at the next practice. Then leave your instrument in a safe but accessible place with the music stand loaded with the next day's study material open at the required page. This takes away one decision to be made the next practice. It takes some discipline to get this routine started, but is certainly worth a try.

Surprisingly, perhaps, in my experience the families who get the most done are often those in which both parents are working and there are several children. They are the ones who know they have to plan their time to use it efficiently, and focus the child's attention in order to get the practice done.

Factors affecting children's motivation

Where parents have high expectations and attribute possible success to effort rather than to ability, they are themselves motivated to become highly involved in the learning process and, conversely, where parents attribute success to ability, they may be discouraged from participating in learning. Typically, children who stay involved in learning to play an instrument believe that their parents are supportive of this activity; children who give up believe their parents are less supportive.

Parents with broad interests in music

Parents of musically successful children typically have broad interests in music rather than performance expertise, according to research by John Sloboda[16]. Many of the highest rated children in research in the 1990s had developed a very strong sense of themselves as 'musical':

"This seemed to come about through the way in which their early musical achievements were praised and 'made a fuss of' by the immediate family. Such praise came most naturally from parents who were not highly proficient musicians themselves, and who were, therefore, genuinely impressed by their child's modest accomplishments. Even though the notion of 'talent' may have little scientific foundation, belief in one's own talent can be a powerful motivator for the continuing, sometimes gruelling, long-term engagement with practice. Unfortunately, belief that one is not 'talented' can have an opposite negative effect on motivation and effort."

Children's motivation and enjoyment are affected by many factors, including the repertoire they study, their view of ability and effort, their teachers, and their parents. High levels of support and challenge have a positive effect on teenagers in all areas of skill. Parents of accomplished children typically:

- devote great amounts of time and energy to meeting the needs of their children
- set high standards
- encourage productive use of time
- provide challenging opportunities
- make sure lessons and materials are available
- set aside areas of the home where their children can work privately.

This support needs to be there constantly to create a good learning environment with a pleasant, relaxed, optimistic atmosphere. Indeed, many fine musicians say they would have given up had it not been for the support they received when young from their parents. Conversely, in later years, people who did not persevere may reproach their parents with comments such as "Why didn't you make me practise?".

Deliberate and incidental practice

In the 1990s, two sorts of practice were distinguished by Anders Ericsson and his colleagues: *deliberate* and *incidental*[3]. *Deliberate* practice is where the pupil pursues a specific pattern of scales, studies, pieces, and so on, with a view to improving expertise. This is needed for progress to be made at any stage, and it seems that the amount of this sort of practice is finally what distinguishes the high fliers from the others.

Incidental practice includes the playing that is done in groups – eg bands, ensembles and orchestras – and is also extremely useful. It has the advantage of increasing playing hours. It also gives pupils experience of different teachers and methods and introduces them to such concepts of ensemble playing as following a leader or conductor, counting, and keeping one's place even when not playing all the notes. These group sessions give youngsters an opportunity to fill in gaps in their knowledge and to allow previously only half-grasped concepts to be consolidated. Playing in groups is very useful in the development of sight reading skills – those who play only alone are more likely to have problems with reading at sight. The social element of group work is, of course, also very important.

Incidental practice may also include solo work – playing through past repertoire, playing by ear, improvising, playing folk music, Christmas carols, etc. In this way pupils can develop fluency at their instrument, they can teach themselves about different styles, and learn to listen for interesting harmonies, melodies and rhythms. The benefits of generally 'messing around' at an instrument include a healthy attitude towards music-making, which may lead to increased motivation for further *deliberate* practice.

An ensemble activity may possibly give rise to what has been described by Susan Hallam as a *crystallising experience*[6]. This may be a single event, be it a live concert, recording, TV programme, playing experience, or lesson with a special teacher, which can provide a child with the intrinsic motivation essential for pursuing the amount of practice needed to gain real expertise on an instrument.

Flexibility but focus

All children are individual and have their own practice requirements. What suits one child may well not suit siblings. For example, one child may wish to be at the centre of things, surrounded by adoring members of the family who applaud every scrape and squeak, whereas others may prefer to be left alone to sort things out for themselves. These wishes should be respected unless a parent suspects the practice is not going well, in which case some sort of compromise needs to be struck. Maybe a private concert at the end of the week, or a shared five minutes at the end of each session, could be suggested for the child who likes to practise alone.

Precious time may be wasted fussing over stands, reeds and other paraphernalia, and this should be discouraged. Although parents should not intrude unnecessarily or excessively, it is advisable to have a realistic picture of what actually happens at practice time, otherwise there may be a huge discrepancy between expectation and reality.

Typical practice sessions?

A study of children's practice behaviour was carried out in Australia by a group of psychologists[17]. This followed 158 primary school children during their first three years of instrumental study, and involved talking to parents, teachers and pupils about their practice. Video recordings were made, at intervals, of these practice sessions, and a detailed study made of three selected children, aged nine and ten.

Whilst acknowledging that a video practice session will not necessarily be a completely true representation of a normal one, these three pupils nevertheless demonstrated some interesting behaviours. Particularly notable was the amount of time wasted. For instance, many minutes were wasted with protracted preparation – taking out music and finding the appropriate pages, getting the seat to the right height, organising something to prop the music on, oiling trumpet valves, and even telling a pet bird which was flying around to "Stay in one place or I'll ground you for the day", and later enquiring of it "Did you like that tune?". History does not relate the reply!

Pieces and scales were generally played through, possibly twice by the more diligent, but with no correction of errors, and sometimes to comments like "I hate that one" and "Why do I have to do this stupid stuff?".

All parents were around, some more involved than others, all seemingly familiar with the idea of practice, but none employing any strategies which would make the practice effective relative to the time spent on it. At the end of each session, effusive praise was given regardless of progress made, or lack of it. Most sadly, very little enjoyment was derived by anyone but, in each and every case, the involved parties believed that practice had been done and that was good enough!

How parents can help

Learning to practise effectively is a skill in itself. Researchers suggest that the highest levels of performance result from the best training conditions and learning environments[18]. In contrast to many sports in which the coach is often present during practice, music students usually practise on their own. Indeed, they often have individual instrumental lessons, reflecting the fact that practising and performing are very often solo rather than group or team activities.

There are boring, tedious, ineffective ways of practising, and there are challenging, varied and efficient ways of practising. Often it is not easy for the student to devise effective practice strategies to overcome technical and musical problems. Teachers can advise in lessons, but they are not available to help during practice periods. Sometimes parents wish to help their children, but are not sure of the best ways of helping, or sometimes they feel that, as they have no knowledge of music, they would not be able to assist.

Early help to promote good progress through good practice should enable the pupil to develop intrinsic motivation later on. This means that, in the same way as a good teacher's main aim is eventually to make themselves redundant (because the pupil is able to learn new music entirely by themselves), so parents who have given their time and support generously in the early years may hope to reap the benefits of a self-motivated musician.

Many research studies have demonstrated that parental involvement is critical to children's musical achievement. One such major research project was carried out in the 1990s by a team led by John Sloboda at Keele University (see box below).

High achieving children and parental support

A study of 257 children and their parents found that the most musically able children had the highest levels of parental support[10]. The teacher-parent interaction was found to be of critical importance. They found that the most successful children had parents who took notes during lessons, spoke to the teacher at the end of the lesson, and supervised practice. The highest achieving children received the most support from their parents up to the age of 11. Thereafter parental support diminished as the children were increasingly driven by intrinsic motives to practise regularly by themselves.

Once children start learning an instrument, Sloboda and his colleagues believe parental involvement is often critical as to whether the child persists or gives up. They believe that high levels of musical achievement are likely to be unattainable without supportive parental involvement. They also claim that the more crucial determinant of the musical achievement of children is not the musical literacy of the parents, but rather the level of support and time commitment which the parents are willing and able to make. Parental involvement in the early stages of instrumental learning is thought to be a better predictor of student achievement than other factors such as musical aptitude test results.

There are a few children who seem to have a natural instinct for music, who are going to be exceptional on an instrument whatever the circumstances – however much or little they are surrounded by music, however much or little parental support they get, and however good or poor their teachers are. However, for the vast majority of children, their progress and achievement will be determined by the support they get from their environment – from home and at school, from their teachers, friends and family.

My own research has shown that parents do not need to be musical, or have musical skills, to be able to help their children[15]. Parents can assist their children in learning a musical instrument by surrounding their children with music (eg playing recordings of music and taking their children to musical events), and by encouraging and praising them. Parents may listen to their young child's music lesson and be in the same room to encourage their child when practising. Or they may take notes during the lesson, and ask their child questions and guide the practice at home. Some parents try to learn the basics of reading music notation, and aim to play very simple duets with their offspring. These are all different and effective ways of being involved.

Parents and teachers want children to learn to love and enjoy music. Progress when practising often seems slow (or even non-existent!) to the student. When parents appreciate and enjoy every small step of their children's practice, they can tell them regularly the good things they see and hear, eg "Do you remember two weeks ago you couldn't do this bit at all? Now it sounds lovely!". Children are motivated to practise because they receive lots of encouragement from their parents and teachers, in lessons, ensembles, music workshops and concerts. Group activities motivate children, especially playing together, hearing more advanced pupils, and making friends. Attendance at music courses is much to be encouraged.

In the early stages, parental support is one of the most influential factors in helping to build a good practice foundation. A parent with enough information to monitor whether the child is doing the right thing is a great asset. As technique develops, as reading ability progresses and as confidence is gained, practices will require less parental input, though praise and encouragement are always beneficial and will be needed for many years.

Supporting your child

Listening
- ❑ Surround your children with music from the earliest possible age by singing with them and playing recordings of good music.
- ❑ Buy recordings of the best performances of classical music, especially instrumental, choral and orchestral music by composers such as Bach, Mozart and Beethoven, so that your child has a concept of the aesthetic beauty of music (see *Listening to music* on page 34 for suggestions).
- ❑ Take your child to children's concerts, having first purchased and listened to recordings.

Equipment
- ❑ Provide a good instrument with a suitable stool or chair, and a music stand if necessary, for practice.

Lessons
- ❑ Arrange instrumental lessons with a good teacher.
- ❑ Take your child to music lessons.
- ❑ Consider staying to listen to lessons, if the teacher agrees.
- ❑ Be chauffeur to and from rehearsals.

Participation
- ❑ Encourage participation in concerts, festivals, music courses, sponsored practices, and so on, to motivate and inspire your child.
- ❑ Attend your child's concerts and performances whenever possible.

Encouragement
- ❑ Be willing to find out what is needed at different stages.
- ❑ Keep up, if possible, in the early stages, to be able to distinguish correct from incorrect.
- ❑ Constantly give encouragement.
- ❑ Praise when appropriate.
- ❑ Provide incentives when necessary.
- ❑ Put things into perspective when necessary.
- ❑ Be respectful of the high profile that music lessons and music practice need to be given.

Working with your child

Some parents may wish to attend lessons and practise regularly with their child. If the parent is able and the teacher is willing, parents can take notes during lessons to help with practice at home. The more detail that is written down, the more it will help jog the parent's memory (and the child's) as to *which* sections are to be practised, *why* they are to be practised, and *how* they are to be practised (see *From a parent's notebook* below).

From a parent's notebook

RH = right hand
LH = left hand
HT = hands together

Detailed notes taken by parent during piano lesson	*Brief notes made by parent after lesson*
Scales and arpeggios	
G major scale – *2 8ves*	
Notes good	
LH fingering unsure – *1 on D on way down*	*Scale*
Practise 1 8ve only:	*G maj 1 8ve*
LH descending 4x	*LH down 4x, 1 on D*
LH up + down 4x slowly, big rich tone on each note	*LH 4x up + down, slow, big tone*
RH 2x	*RH 2x*
HT 4x	*HT 4x*
G major arpeggio	*Arp*
Good fingering	*G maj*
Practise awkward interval of 4th – seesaw	*D – G LH 10x*
D – G – D – G each hand 10x	*RH 10x*
Reading	*Reading*
Excellent rhythm – kept going very well!	
Each day play a new sight reading piece	
Look at it – examine it	*Look – mime – sing – play*
Mime it	*(keep going)*
Sing it	
Play it, keeping going come what may	
Extract one awkward note, interval, bar or passage and practise it	*Practise awkward passage*
(slowly, out of rhythm if necessary, separately if appropriate)	
Play piece again, concentrating on expressive dynamics	*Play – dynamics*
Work again on one awkward passage	*Practise awkward bit*
Play again concentrating on character of piece	*Play – character*
Then play straight through yesterday's reading piece	*Play yesterday's piece*

Beethoven Sonatina referred to opposite in ***From a parent's notebook***

Sonatina in G: 1st mov

Beethoven

From a parent's notebook (continued)

<u>*Beethoven Sonatina in G 1ˢᵗ mov*</u>	<u>*Beethoven 1*</u>
Newest piece (see opposite page)	
Phrases already becoming well shaped –	
now exaggerate even more	
Play RH bars 5+6+1ˢᵗ note of bar 7 with	
cresc from low G to top G 4x	*RH 5+6-7 cresc 4x*
Then 5+6-7 HT 4x	*HT 5+6-7 cresc 4x*
Again dynamics:	
Play RH 25-28 mf and cresc up	
arpeggio 2x	*RH 25-28 mf + cresc 2x*
Try RH 29-32 as an echo – but still a	*29-32 echo + cresc 2x*
little cresc up arp 2x	
HT 25-28 mf 2x	*HT 25-28 2x*
HT 29-32 echo 2x	*29-32 2x*
HT 25-32 mf + echo2x	*25-32 2x*
Fingering good except:	
Check LH bar 9 – 3 on F♯, not 2	
Play LH bars 9+10 2x	*LH 9+10 2x 3 on F♯*
LH bar 8+1ˢᵗ beat bar 9 4x	*8-9 4x*
LH bars 8-10 2x	*8-10 2x*
HT bars 9-10 2x	*HT 9+10 2x*
HT bar 8+1ˢᵗ beat bar 9 4x	*8-9 4x*
Finally HT bars 8-10 2x	*8-10 2x*
<u>*Long long ago*</u>	<u>*LLA*</u>
Revision piece (see next page)	
Beautiful singing sound in RH – very good	
Can the LH be even softer?	*Softer LH*
Mime LH 1 bar only 2x	*1 bar only – 1, 2, 3, 4, 7, 8, 9*
Play that 1 bar with big singing RH	*Mime LH – add RH*
over mimed LH	
Then 1 bar LH very softly – doesn't	*Hardly sounding LH –*
matter if some notes don't sound	*add RH*
Add RH for that 1 bar	
Play 1 bar LH very soft but trying to	*Very soft LH – add RH*
make all notes sound	
Add RH for that 1 bar	
Each day work on a different bar, eg bar 1,	
2, 3, 4, 7, 8 or 9	
Then play whole phrase, concentrating on	*Play whole phrase*
soft LH	
Then play whole piece	*Play whole piece*

Long Long Ago referred to on previous page in *From a parent's notebook*

When young children are practising on their own, it can be helpful if parents attend lessons and make weekly practice charts for them to follow. Or parents can record the lesson, so the child can hear again their own playing in the lesson, and the sounds and rhythms of the teacher's demonstrations, and be reminded of the way in which the teacher approached a particular point. The parent's role in the lesson is that of a silent observer, taking notes to help with practising at home, asking questions only when something is not clear, but not making comments on the child's performance unless their views are solicited.

Many people find being a parent one of the most difficult and challenging jobs they have ever tackled. Parents who want to practise with their children need to learn how to work at home with them – not to scold or get angry or frustrated with their children, but rather to assist by setting a good example in planning the practice, by praising and by encouraging.

We all, adults as well as children, respond far more positively to a suggestion if we have first received praise for what we have done. If we encounter criticism, we feel unhappy and blank, and tend to resist further input. Children will be more motivated to practise if their efforts, however poor, are met with enthusiasm and understanding. Parents need to express their love through patience, kindness and respect towards their children. This will help to develop a close relationship between the parent and child, which is a reward in itself. Parents need to provide a quiet, positive, loving environment in which their children's abilities can be developed (see *Sample conversations between parent and child* opposite).

Sample conversations between parent and child

*Arising from lesson noted in **From a parent's notebook** on page 27*

Understanding parent
Parent: Ali liked your scales last week. She wants you to get your fingering more secure. Can you play the left hand of G major – just one octave?
Child plays.
Parent: That sounded excellent! Was the fingering right?
Child: No, I think something went wrong going down.
Parent: Can you work out what it should be? What finger do you need on the D?
Child: I think it should be a 4.
Parent: Try it then.
Child plays.
Parent: Are you supposed to end with a finger 4?
Child: No! I don't think so.
Parent: How about trying a thumb on the D?
Child plays.
Parent: Great! Did that work?
Child: Yes!
Parent: Play that again – left hand, one octave, just going down.
Child plays.
Parent: Was that good?
Child: Yes!
Parent: Good. Now play that one octave up <u>and</u> down.
Child plays.
Parent: Super. What did Ali say about the sound?
Child: A big sound.
Parent: Exactly. Now you've sorted out the fingering, play that three more times, very slowly, with a big sound on each note.

The parent is supportive and understanding, questioning the child, developing the child's ability to work along the lines indicated by the teacher. The parent doesn't have to know anything about music other than what has been observed in the lesson. The scene is set for achievement and success.

Demoralising parent
Parent: OK. Scales. G major. Fingering not good. Left hand must have 1 on D. Play it.
Child plays.
Parent: Deep sigh of frustration. No, that's not right. I said ONE on D.
Child plays again – with 1 correctly on D.
Parent: Why's it so uneven? Play like this. *Parent taps out pulse.*
Child tries to play with parent's beat, but now misses finger 1 on D.
The child begins to get upset, and feels s/he can neither play the correct fingering nor play evenly. The parent can't understand why the child can't do two such simple things at the same time.

This critical, demoralising, unsympathetic environment is not good for progress.

Children usually like their lessons but not always the practice. It is vital to understand that, if practice is poor, children merely learn to develop their faults, which is worse than not practising at all as far as progress is concerned, and offers little or no personal satisfaction. Parents can try to make each practice session a pleasant, cosy time together. They can shape and guide the practice, offering plenty of encouragement and moral support. Supervising practices requires skill, tact, perseverance and imagination. Children's learning flourishes with gentle guidance, no criticism and plenty of praise.

Guiding your child's practice

Timing

- ❑ With very young children, practices need to be very short, but must be regular and frequent.

- ❑ Try practising at the same time each day.

- ❑ Consider practising in the morning when the mind is fresh and uncluttered by encounters of the day.

Planning

- ❑ Plan what will be practised – both the order of technical exercises, scales, sight reading, pieces, and so on, and which part of each exercise, scale, reading, piece – but then be flexible.

- ❑ Discuss with your child what is to be done and how, and guide the practice accordingly.

- ❑ Children get frustrated when asked to stop in the middle of a piece. Either practise assigned sections, or let them play straight through the piece (or one followed by the other).

- ❑ Parents need to use their imagination at practices, eg boredom sets in when there is too much playing straight through pieces and not enough working on specific points.

- ❑ Your child may like to do some part of the practice alone. Discuss it with your child, and then with the teacher.

See also **Structuring practice sessions** on page 48.

Environment

- ❑ Use a lively tone of voice during your children's practice – a gentle, enthusiastic manner can encourage them in their efforts.

- ❑ Give plenty of praise.

- ❑ Don't move goalposts – if working on something and it improves, praise it – don't sigh and complain that now something else is wrong. When asked to concentrate on something fresh, a previously correct aspect may go adrift. Come back to that point later after working at the new point.

- ❑ You'll have more patience if you set your expectations at a reasonable level.

- ❑ Make the practice environment as comfortable as possible – battling against the television or computer games, or other children playing noisily nearby, is not conducive to good learning.

- ❑ If necessary, reward siblings if they are quiet during practice time.

Engagement

❑ Record your child's practice and play it back to your child and/or teacher.

❑ Each week arrange for your child to perform a short concert for members of the family who do not normally hear the practice.

❑ Always end the practice positively – stop when all is going well, then your child will be eager to practise again – one successful practice leads to another.

❑ Often the more proficient children become, the more willing they are to practise – it's a question of getting through the less rewarding initial stages.

❑ Stimulate your child's natural desire to learn – eventually practice needs to be made interesting rather than fun.

See also *Getting motivated* on page 83.

Making music in the du Pré family

Hilary du Pré, sister of Jacqueline, gives a wonderful description of her early years' music-making in her book *A Genius in the Family*[19]. Their mother was a professional pianist and piano teacher and was trained in Dalcroze (responding to music with movement). Hilary, too, became a fine musician and teacher.

"From as early as I can remember, Mum entertained us with music. She was always singing, playing the piano, clapping and stepping rhythms. Music was a wonderful game. As she played, we would skip and dance around the room, making shapes in the air according to the phrase shapes. We curled into the tiniest forms when the music was soft, and burst out jumping into the air when it was loud. We tiptoed and crouched for creepy music and skipped to dotted rhythms. We had to convey ferocity or tragedy and all as a spontaneous reaction to her playing.

"When I was four, Mum started to teach me the piano. I would clamber on to the piano stool and line my tummy button up to middle C. My piano book with its black and white giraffes had something new on every page. Each time I mastered a piece with correctly shaped hands and fingering, I performed it from memory to Mum, Dad, Mrs Latimer, our next-door neighbour – and sometimes the milkman. When Gran and Auntie Em were staying, we had a concert every evening after tea. I loved the performing, the delight it seemed to give, and being told to learn the next piece quickly ready for another concert.

"When learning a new piece, I wasn't allowed to look at my fingers, but had to concentrate on looking ahead at the music. However, when playing from memory, I could watch my fingers as much as I liked. Mum would talk to me about the contrast between making big sounds and little sounds, encouraging me to be aware of the different touches. I had to listen very carefully as every piece had to tell a story.

"Playing the piano became second nature to me. I loved it and took it completely for granted. It was my time with Mum and she always seemed pleased with me, stopping anything she was doing to come and listen."

Listening to music

Children's aural (listening) abilities are well developed before birth, while motor skills are developed by around the age of three, but visual skills (for reading) not until about the age of seven. Make the most of young children's aural ability and let them listen to good music from as early an age as possible. Before starting to learn an instrument, it helps if children have music in their ears, their heads and their hearts. Let them be inspired by beautiful sounds. Like learning a language, it is easier if one hears the music before and while studying it. Learning a language purely from a textbook would be much more difficult (and less enjoyable) than if one were surrounded by the sound of the new language. Furthermore, it would be impossible to get the pronounciation right. Children are more likely to wish to participate in music-making themselves if inspired by the music they hear around them.

Find recordings of the pieces being studied or, if not the actual pieces, then other pieces by the same composer. Listen to as many different interpretations as possible, and compare and contrast them. The great Russian teacher, Heinrich Neuhaus said to a conservatoire student who brought a Rachmaninov recording and asked for advice: "Listen to your record 10 or 20 times, then I shall hear you *once* to hear to what good effect this listening to music has had on you". He continued: "Recordings are now probably the most powerful means of education" (quoted by Anne Turner in *The Whole Child*[20]).

- ❏ Let children listen to fine performances by top performers so they can identify good quality sound when they hear it and know what to aim for in their own playing. Encourage them to listen to as much music as possible and help them learn to discern between good and less good performances.

- ❏ Play music to children at mealtimes, bedtime, playtime, in the car, and so on.

- ❏ Listen to good radio programmes such as Radio 3 and/or Classic FM to hear a wide variety of music.

- ❏ Build up a collection of recordings and/or borrow them from your local library.

- ❏ Listen to plenty of solo music of your child's instrument (including sonatas and concertos), but also orchestral music (for sounds of different instruments) and choral music (for singing sounds).

- ❏ Listen to other music by composers currently being studied. For instance, if your child is studying a piece by a 20th century Spanish composer, listen to other music by the same composer, or from the same country, or the same period.

- ❏ Take your child to live performances – your child will remember the excitement of an outing. However, avoid putting young children off by taking them to long concerts late in the evening. Try to locate children's concerts in your area, short lunchtime concerts, afternoon or early evening concerts. If a late evening concert is the only option, then consider attending the first half and going home at the interval. Listen beforehand to recordings of the music to be performed so the programme is familiar and even more enjoyable for you and your child.

Suggested listening

Start by listening to some of the following but, obviously, the list is endless:

Bach	Violin concertos Brandenburg concertos
Haydn	Piano sonatas String quartets
Mozart	Piano sonatas Piano concertos Operas, eg The Marriage of Figaro
Beethoven	Piano sonatas Piano concertos Symphonies
Schubert	Lieder
Brahms	Symphonies
Tchaikovsky	Piano concertos Violin concerto
Dvorak	Symphonies, eg No 9: New World Cello concerto
Elgar	Cello concerto
Debussy	Preludes (for piano) La Mer (for orchestra) Pelleas et Melisande (opera)
Bartok	String quartets Violin concertos Piano concertos
Stravinsky	The Firebird (for orchestra)
Shostakovitch	Symphonies, especially No 5 String quartets
World music	eg Indian, African

Ask your music teacher for further recommendations.

Chapter 2: Teachers

First and foremost, teachers will aim to inspire their pupils and foster their intrinsic motivation. Once pupils are inspired, teachers will want to show them how best to develop their musicality at their chosen instrument.

Teaching why to practise

It is important for teachers to consider how the notion of practice is presented to new pupils and the parents of young pupils. To uninitiated parents and new students, ie those who have not themselves had the experience of learning to play a musical instrument, regular practice may not be such an obvious requirement as it is to teachers and playing parents. It is essential that teachers explain why practice is so important. Playing an instrument is a complicated business. The mechanics of playing must become automatic alongside learning to play musically and expressively. Learning to read music is, in itself, a difficult task and, again, needs much practice to develop fluency. Explain that if any complex skill were practised for only thirty minutes for each of thirty weeks of the year, then expertise would be negligible even after a number of years. It is important to make children and parents aware that learning to play a musical instrument requires discipline and effort. It is not an 'easy ride'.

Teaching how to practise

When one considers that the ratio of practice time to lesson time is, on average, about 5:1, it becomes evident that a fair proportion of each lesson should, ideally, be devoted to the matter of practice. This time may consist of a demonstration of practice techniques, verbal discussion about how to approach practice, and role reversal whereby the pupil becomes teacher and explains how a specific piece or exercise might be approached. The way students practise is influenced more by what teachers *do* in the lesson, for instance demonstrating a technique or getting a student to try a particular approach, than by what they *say*.

> *Tell me and I'll forget,*
> *Show me and I may remember,*
> *Involve me and I'll understand.*
> *Confucius*

The Danish piano teacher Esther Lund Madsen has a simple but effective teaching technique: **praise – improve – praise**. After hearing a young child play a piece, she will praise some aspect of the performance. She may then ask "Was it good? Can it be better? Of course, one can always play better!". She then suggests an improvement and demonstrates it. The child's imitation of the demonstration is then duly praised. She will ask the child how they should practise, eg slowly and hands separately, and *ask the child to do it for her in the lesson*.

Many teachers will ask their pupils, after hearing a piece in lesson, "Tell me what you thought was good about your performance" which immediately encourages pupils to think positively before discussing areas for improvement. Other teachers will ask "*How* do you practise that?", which is the question pupils must constantly be asking themselves during their practice sessions.

Encouraging effective practice

With the best will in the world, unless pupils know how and why to practise, rather than what and for how long, practice is going to be far from ideal and effective. One of the teacher's main tasks to give pupils enough confidence to feel that they can go away, practise, and achieve success in the given task. It is important that the pupil understands the reason for practising a certain passage in a certain way – it is more motivating practising towards a known goal.

If teachers spend a little time at the end of each lesson instructing parents of young children how to practise a particular piece, then the parent will be able to guide the child to follow those instructions during the week, thus making the lesson more valuable. Without this sort of support at home, many children will simply play through the piece from the beginning until they get stuck and then go on to the next piece.

Certainly in the early stages of learning an instrument, it is very helpful if the pupil and parent can leave the lesson knowing that there is one main point to be worked on during the week. This may be posture; it may be an improvement in bowing or breathing technique; it may be a musical issue such as the performance of slurs or *staccato* notes. Whatever the point, pupils need to understand that it should be applied, wherever possible, to every piece/scale/exercise currently being studied. With small children, the point should be emphasised through many repetitions of the task in the lesson.

One of the teacher's tasks is to achieve this while retaining the child's interest. Here is one idea – after two or three repetitions, give the child a short mental task, eg reciting the days of the week backwards, counting in twos or fives, closing their eyes and trying to remember what you are wearing, which distracts them for a moment; then immediately go into more repetitions. It is easy to underestimate what small children can achieve – most of them seem to enjoy these brain teasers, and the mission of repetition is also achieved. Other ideas are to add a piece to a jigsaw, or build a stacking wooden toy, for each repetition.

When the opportunity arises, if there is not another pupil immediately beforehand, ensure you are practising when children arrive for their lessons. Tell them what you are doing, so that they know that you practise. Also find a moment during the lesson to comment on what you are currently working on and casually say "I've done it twenty times, only thirty more to go". Sometimes in a lesson say "Let's do this twelve times for fun" and vary the repetitions, perhaps alternating between the two of you, or timing the process, or putting objects (eg raisins or chocolate buttons) in a line on the window sill so that little ones can *see* how the repetitions look.

Varied practice

The notion of 'varied practice' is an interesting and productive one. Doris da Costa believes that children, particularly younger ones (though this probably applies equally well to less highly motivated older children) will get more out of their practice if they are allowed to choose some interesting ways to do it from a list supplied by their teacher, rather than just routine repetitions[21].

In her experiment there were 28 pupils, aged from eight to 47, playing a variety of instruments. They were allowed to choose to practise either on a conventional scheme of breaking down their music into short phrases and performing a required number of repetitions of each, or else choosing, from a card, five novel ways of approaching the music. The fifth choice was always to play the section from memory; for the other four the selection might include:

- ❏ playing the whole phrase *piano* (softly)
- ❏ playing the whole phrase *forte* (strongly)
- ❏ playing a *crescendo* through each phrase (starting soft and getting stronger)
- ❏ playing a *diminuendo* through each phrase (starting strong and getting softer)
- ❏ playing the phrase *legato* (smoothly)
- ❏ playing the phrase *staccato* (detached)
- ❏ changing the mood of the phrase
- ❏ playing the phrase as a question
- ❏ playing the rhythm of the phrase on one note only.

At the end of a few weeks of choosing, those who had opted for the 'varied practice' said that they had enjoyed their practice more, felt they were able to play more fluently, learned their music faster, improved their technique and were better at memorising. Although this was a small study with a small sample, it suggested that 'varied practice' might be a useful extension to the more conventional type.

Practice sheets or diaries can be useful, especially if reinforced and signed by parents. They probably give a fairly accurate guide as to what is done, but should not be believed entirely. Parents have been known to collude with their children and 'cook the books', not realising how counter-productive this behaviour is. A good way of finding out whether or not a pupil is practising at home is to ask the pupil to memorise a passage or piece for the next lesson.

Unusual challenges, such as "Over the holidays please listen to recordings of as many different concertos on your instrument as possible and next lesson play by ear one section (only a few notes if a beginner) of a favourite movement", may have a dramatic effect on motivating some pupils. As a teacher, try to discover which pupils are inspired by what sort of challenge.

If practice at home is obviously not going well, despite discussing it at length with a pupil, ask the child (or child's parent) to make a recording (either video or audio) of a practice. Watching or listening to this will enable you to give well-informed and helpful advice to the child to improve the quality and value of practice sessions.

Developing pupils' independence

The practice needs of each pupil change constantly, working from much repetition in the early stages to speed along the process of elementary automation – note reading, breathing, bowing technique, finger patterns, hand co-ordination, and so on – to more analytical and intellectual practice later. At the same time, one hopes that a process of transfer from extrinsic to intrinsic motivation is slowly taking place. In the very early years, most of the energy for practice may come from the parent(s) and teacher(s) but later on, as the teenage years approach, the responsibility should transfer to the pupil.

Not only do teachers need to assist students to acquire musical expertise, they need to help them become independent learners, aiding them plan their practice, suggesting they study and analyse their scores, rehearse mentally (away from the instrument) as well as physically (at the instrument), and listen to high quality performances. Pupils can be invited to choose the pieces they will learn, or the composers of the pieces, and to decide how they are going to tackle them. Practice notebooks can be written by the pupil rather than the teacher, although the disadvantage of this is the increase in time required. While teachers can jot down notes as the pupil is playing, pupils need to stop, put instruments down, find a surface to write on, etc, and all this takes valuable time from the lesson. However, in the interest of pupils taking responsibility for themselves, it may be worth it.

Every teacher's goal is to make themselves redundant – to put their pupils in a position where they can continue to learn on their own. This is done by teaching principles, so what is taught about one bar or phrase, eg of a Bach minuet, can be applied generally throughout the piece, or to any other minuet, to any other similar dance movement, or even any other piece by Bach. Likewise, when discussing how to practise a certain passage, the pupil needs to be aware that this principle can be applied to other similar passages (see *How to practise two specific pieces* on page 59).

Targets

Both short-term and long-term goals need to be considered with regard to practice. Short-term goals may go no further than helping the pupil persevere through a difficult period. This may include the promise of starting a new music book if they finish a particular piece, learning a duet with a friend, performing at a concert or festival, preparing for an exam, or joining an orchestra or other ensemble. Sometimes a talk about responsibility combined with discussing musical targets and timetables and ways of practising will motivate a flagging interest. Long-term goals tie in with pupil (or sometimes, teacher) aspirations – whether the ultimate goal is perhaps to play professionally or fulfil some other high profile aim, or just to enjoy playing and have some musical fun. Whatever the motive, the teacher's aim is a dual one of balancing enjoyment with achievement, and practice needs to reflect this. Teachers need to ensure their pupils see the connection between practice and progress. Good practice needs to be rewarded, encouraged, discussed, and never taken for granted.

To motivate pupils by giving them a target, organise regular pupils' concerts in a non-competitive environment with a friendly atmosphere. Every pupil plays a prepared piece. Try to involve pupils in ensemble playing – duets and trios, or including other instruments. Ensure concerts are always followed by food – it is what the children enjoy and remember, and what makes it worth their while coming and playing. The more delicious the food, the better the concert, in their opinion! Ask each pupil's family to bring something for a party afterwards.

Encourage families to arrange their own informal concerts. Every Saturday evening children could perform their favourite pieces or their complete repertoire. Or encourage two or three of your pupils' families to have an afternoon concert at one of their houses. Everyone brings something delicious for tea afterwards.

Inspire your pupils with fine music by organising a concert outing. Encourage pupils to listen in advance to recordings of the music in the programme so it will be familiar to them, which will enhance their enjoyment of the concert.

Expectations

While teachers need to have high expectations – for *all* children have great potential – each child needs to be treated as an individual. It is worth considering whether each pupil at any one time comes into the category of needing a challenge or needing to be reassured. With the former category, teachers need to provide lots of new material which pushes the boundaries either technically or musically (or both). The latter group will, inevitably, move more slowly and cautiously and thrive on repetition of pieces well within their capability – challenges will need to be approached with great care and timed with delicacy. In other words, some children will welcome clear challenges; others need easily attainable goals to build their confidence. In all cases, build your pupils' self-esteem by emphasising their strong points. Praise and encourage them – let them know you are proud of them.

Communication with parents

Communication with parents is very important in order to develop a good working relationship. Consider circulating a termly newsletter including not only dates of lessons, ensemble classes and concerts, but also gems of wisdom to encourage families. Lend parents relevant books and articles about music-making and practising. Talk individually to parents about progress. Encourage them to tell you if problems arise with practising. Ask them to talk to another parent whose child may have had the same problem – in the telling the problem may resolve itself. Assure parents that progress includes studying pieces in greater depth, not just moving onto more difficult pieces.

Chapter 3: Pupils

Practise for progress and pleasure

So you have decided to learn an instrument, and you have chosen the one you like. In order to develop your skill, to learn and memorise music, and to prepare for performance, you will need to practise. And the more progress you hope to make, the more you will need to practise. Practice makes certain elements of playing an instrument automatic, so you can concentrate on playing musically – playing expressively – communicating the composer's meaning to your audience. To make good progress you will need to practise regularly – every day; and you will need to practise effectively.

Before you leave your lesson, always make sure you have a clear idea of *what* you are to practise, *why* you are to practise it, and *how* you are to do it. If in doubt, ask. Good practice increases the chances of things going well. Careful, focused practice almost always leads to progress. Progress leads to pleasure and satisfaction – for you, your teacher, your parents, perhaps also your friends and wider family. Trust your teacher and trust yourself.

Approach to practising

Someone needs to be responsible for practice being done. If you are very young, you might like a practice-companion – someone to help you with your practice. If you are older, you may well prefer peace and quiet without being disturbed. It may be a good idea to have an in-between period when a parent is present for the last five minutes of practice time, or for the first practice after your lesson each week and/or the last practice before your next lesson. Or arrange a performance for the family each time you have mastered a piece of music. All this depends on family life but, provided you are taking responsibility for your own practice, you should be able to choose the environment you would like, within reasonable limits.

Practising need not be a chore. Your challenge is to make your practice interesting. For instance, playing straight through what you can play of your pieces gets boring after a while, and also you won't make much progress that way. Work out, perhaps together with your teacher, what part of the piece needs practising, why it needs practising, and how to practise it. Repetition is an important part of practice. Your challenge is learning how to make the repetitions productive. Decide how many repetitions are required, of how short a section, and how to vary the repetitions so you keep listening to what you are playing and continue to improve your playing.

Practice should be a continuation of the lesson, during which you assign yourself specific tasks and supervise your own work. You need to remain mentally alert through the whole of your practice session. When the mind wanders, practice lacks direction and becomes a waste of time and effort. Mistakes can be repeated again and again, so one can get very good at playing poorly. However, if you work carefully every day, constantly engaging both the brain and the ear, you will make good progress. Practice may not make perfect, but it will ensure progress.

Over time you need to build a repertoire of different strategies to deal with different problems, for example:

- ❑ working on difficult passages and practising them slowly

- ❑ practising sections in different rhythms

- ❑ practising with separate bows/tongued

- ❑ practising the bowing only (right hand) or fingering only (left hand) on a string instrument

- ❑ practising hands separately on a keyboard instrument (feet alone, too, on an organ)

- ❑ practising at different speeds

- ❑ exaggerating the dynamic contrasts.

You may find it helpful to have your own practice book, make your own notes in it, and refer to it at every practice. Or you may prefer to write reminders to yourself on the score. You may like to devise a colour code for marking up features such as *legato/staccato, piano/forte, sforzando, crescendo/diminuendo*, etc, as a colour can act as an instant reminder.

A specific routine for practice is not an absolute necessity, but it does ensure that practice gets done as opposed to not done. If you miss a day's practice, it seems more difficult to get down to it the next day. You have to spend longer reminding yourself what you are doing and how you are working on your pieces. Previous progress seems diluted. Try to practise a little each day. Have a regular daily time-slot for your practice and, when you have done it, give yourself a reward, eg a drink of fruit juice, or allow yourself to read another chapter of your favourite book.

Practising for the very young

When you are very young, your parents may explain to you how and what to practise. They may be with you some or all of the time, or at least be around. Ideally, you will agree on a time and place every day, and each do your very best to to keep to the plan. Between you, you may decide to have a reward system with stars or ticks, maybe, and at a given stage a small reward may be earned. Or you may like to organise a family concert or play your instrument at school or church or at a local club.

Ten tips for carefree cello practice

by Georgia Clemson, age 7, whose mother used to supervise her practices, and who is now a fine teenage cellist (her sister is a good violinist, too!)[22]

1 Don't let your sister come in and annoy you whilst you're in the middle of a piece.
2 Make sure you play it perfectly straight away – then you won't have to play it over and over again.
3 Keep some chocolate handy, in case you feel peckish (it is best not to let your mum know about this bit).
4 Always try and keep calm in a crisis (eg especially when your bow gets stuck in the strings)!
5 Make sure you've got ear plugs and a crash hat for when your mum forgets to keep calm!

6   Always know what YOU want to practise – this may be very different from what your mum wants you to do.

7   Make sure you have a good story to tell your mum to distract her from a tricky bit (eg when Mary got locked in the loo at school).

8   Remember your mum is a better mum if she is happy!

9   Make sure your mum makes careful notes in your lesson and doesn't doze off to sleep; it's bound to be your fault if you go wrong later on at home.

10   Have fun playing the cello!

.... *for the slightly older*

As you get older, your parents will be around less – you will be quite capable, with your teacher, of organising your own practice schedule and strategies. You will know what to do and how to do it, but will still welcome constructive comments from other people and enjoy praise when it is due (but not when it isn't!). You may well be very pleased for a taxi service at this stage as, hopefully, you will begin to get involved with other players and join bands, orchestras or other appropriate groups.

.... *for teenagers*

As you approach your teenage years, independence will strike you. You will probably want to sort out your playing by yourself and appreciate a quiet room to yourself – time and space to do things in your own way, to grind away at technical problems and to explore self-expression. Set yourself manageable targets, feel pleased when you achieve them, set yourself further targets, and enjoy your music-making!

.... *and for adults*

As an adult you will be practising because you really want to – for your own pleasure and satisfaction. You are likely to be entirely self-motivated. The problem will not be preferring to do other things, but finding the time to get to your instrument, in between work and other (eg family) commitments. Some of the time at your instrument you will wish to relax and unwind after a hard day or week at work. Some of the time you may wish or need to learn new material, or bring a piece up to performing standard (eg to play with friends in a chamber ensemble) and you will want to make as good use as possible of your limited time.

Observation of lessons

Some teachers are happy for pupils to observe each others' lessons. There are many benefits to arriving early for a music lesson or staying on afterwards to observe other lessons:

- ❑ *Musical* – you can pick up musical points which are sometimes easier to see or hear with another pupil; you can be more receptive when not in the hot-seat!

- ❑ *Technical* – you may pick up extra tips on how to practise, or how to approach a particular problem.

- ❑ *Social* – possibly none of your friends or colleagues plays an instrument, so it is important that you feel part of your music teacher's group – it helps prevent a feeling of isolation (especially for pianists).

❑ ***Inspiration and motivation*** – sometimes one hears someone else playing a piece and decides "I *can* play that piece" or "I can't wait until *I* can play that piece". Although occasionally it can cause momentary distress if someone else plays really well a piece that you are struggling with, usually, in the long term, it spurs one on to greater heights: "If other people can do it, so can I".

Ideally you would stay to observe another pupil who is a little more advanced after your own lesson. Observing a musical pupil can open one's mind to the musical possibilities and stimulate one to work harder.

Having observers in the lesson usually helps those who are having lessons, too. It is good for you to become accustomed to having an audience; it helps you learn to concentrate better; and it encourages good daily practice if you know the results of your practice will be heard by an audience. It also focuses the teacher's attention – they have to make themselves extra clear so everyone can understand the point they are trying to make. So if your teacher encourages it, do go and observe as much as possible, for the good of your fellow pupils as well as of yourselves!

Developing listening skills during practice

A pre-requisite for efficient practice is an honest and objective ear. Without good listening skills, practice can be fruitless. It is easy to hear what you hope to hear, rather than what you actually play. A useful test is to record your playing and listen back to it critically. If the recording is different from what you imagine, more careful listening needs to be done during practice. It is good to experiment with different qualities of sound, exaggerated dynamic levels, and various ways of shaping phrases, to produce different moods and characters in the piece.

Mental practice – practising in your head, away from an instrument – helps develop inner hearing. In your imagination, with no technical problems to confront, you can create and hear the most musical performance possible, which can then influence your performance when at an instrument. Listening skills will also be developed by playing or singing in ensembles, when your own instrument or voice must blend with the others.

Listening to fine performances of wonderful music will awaken your sensitivity to the subtleties of beautiful sound. See list of music in ***Suggested listening*** on page 35.

Section Two

How to practise

Section Two: How to practise

Practice is more effective when musicians plan in advance how they will practise, and carefully assess what they are doing during practice[23]. Relatively short but regular practice sessions are advisable. It helps if students listen to professional recordings and also to teacher demonstrations. Advanced students should study and analyse scores, and practise away from their instrument as well as at their instrument. The old adage 'practice makes perfect' is not necessarily true, because repetition of ineffective practice strategies can yield disappointing results. Achievement is related not only to the length of time spent practising but also to the quality of that practice.

Daniel Coyle, in *The Talent Code*[24], suggests that research over the last decade is debunking the 20th century idea that talent may be mostly genetic. It seems to be much more the case that ability depends on practice – and how one practises. Researchers are now taking more notice of a biological process in which a substance called myelin wraps itself around circuits in the brain. The more the circuits are used, the more myelin grows. Myelin transforms narrow alleys into broad, lightening-fast super-highways. To make myelin, we need to try, we need to make mistakes, we need to try again – and again and again. Daily practice should be challenging. There is no easy way to learn to play a musical instrument (or to become skilled at chess, tennis, or mathematics). But by working at the limits of one's capacity, by extending the boundaries, progress becomes possible for everyone.

William Westney in *The Perfect Wrong Note*[25] urges musicians not to ignore mistakes – they help show what and how to practise. Furthermore, he suggests one helpful way of practising is to make intentional mistakes. For instance, if practising a particular movement to make a particular sound, at first it's more important to get the movement and the sound correct than to aim for the correct note. Successful practising is a creative process. It needn't be predictable or tedious. Being imaginative helps maintain interest and enjoyment.

Chapter 4: Practice strategies

When to practise

Skills developed regularly over a long period of time are retained better than skills developed within a short time period. Regular short practice sessions are generally more effective than fewer longer ones, the ideal length varying with the age and skill level of the musician. Frequent, short practices are best for short, simple tasks and for younger pupils, but longer practice sessions are required for more complex tasks. If practising for long sessions, it is important to take periodic breaks.

It is typically more productive to do two short practices a day than one longer one. Only one very long practice a week, the day before the lesson, is the least good way of working! Ideally, if time permits, it is best to fit in a longer practice in the morning before school or work, and a shorter one in the evening. This may entail going to bed 20 minutes earlier so the alarm can be set 20 minutes earlier in the morning to ensure a good practice before leaving the house. But some people are not at their best early in the morning, and others have to leave the house very early, so evening practices, before or after the evening meal, suit them better.

Structuring practice sessions

If possible, it is good to do the bulk of the serious practice in the morning when one is fresh. Start with technique (warm-ups, scales, arpeggios, exercises and/or studies), followed by sight reading, and continue with detailed work on the newest pieces (working on short sections, slowly, etc) and/or a piece being polished for a forthcoming performance. End with playing through (or working on) some recently learned pieces. This would leave only a small amount of work to be done in the evening, perhaps once through what can be played of the newest piece, working on some recently learned pieces, and perhaps playing some duets or jazz or improvising. Each day everything that has been played or discussed in the lesson should be practised, working in as much detail as possible according to the teacher's suggestions. A good and satisfying practice session involves working diligently on some pieces, and then playing through one or more well-known pieces, thus offering variety.

In the early stages of learning, young beginners may have problems identifying difficult sections and tend to practice by simply playing through the music. They are often unaware of errors. When they can identify errors, they initially deal with them by correcting the single wrong note. Later, small sections (half a bar or a bar) are repeated. As students mature, error correction changes to a focus on difficult sections that are then worked on as units. The ability to identify errors and learn how to deal with them needs to be developed as early as possible.

Students who structure their practice well improve the accuracy and musicality of their performances more than those who practise with no specific structure. A few minutes at the end of one practice planning (and even writing down) what to do at the next practice will result in a much more focused session the next day. However, novice musicians may not have sufficient knowledge to determine the best framework for practice. Good teachers will guide their students by identifying problem areas and discussing effective practice techniques with them. They can help by setting assignments for students to work on, for instance the length of the last note of a piece, accurate rests, a bar with awkward fingering, a big leap, or *staccato* technique. It is important not only to practise the assigned passage, but also to put it into context – start a bar before, then two bars before, then at the beginning of the phrase, each time checking that the awkward passage is still correct.

If you start to get bored during practice, think of a different way of practising. Plan lots of variety. Spend some time learning new notes, some time improving a piece technically and/or musically, some time memorising. Spend part of your practice working on short sections, another part working slowly, another part working hands separately (pianists). Have a goal for each part of your practice. For instance, take one section of your music and improve your *staccato* technique, or develop the dynamics and shaping of phrases, or work on the ornaments. Then explore the likelihood that what works in one piece, eg how to play slurs or *staccato*, may apply in another piece. Optimise your practice time – work out what *not* to practise, and devise ways of improving the difficult passages. Analyse problems and keep trying different strategies to solve them.

Chapter 5: Practising specific issues

Below are some ideas for practising. No-one will agree with every single one of these practice strategies. And not every idea is suitable for every piece. But at some time in my experience as a pupil, a teacher, or an observer on courses and at masterclasses, I have found each of the following strategies to be useful. If the ideas seem to veer on the side of advocating detailed, analytical practice, it's because the majority of young (and not so young) instrumentalists tend to do too much 'playing through' pieces and not enough diagnosing and solving problems. Also, if you're just going to play straight through your pieces, you don't need a book to suggest how to do it!

The essence of practice is dividing the music into logical and manageable chunks for practice, then building it up again into a piece for performance. Strategies need to be devised for practising the difficulties in each short section. This often involves changing some aspect of the music, for instance practising *legato* passages *staccato* (varying the articulation), soft passages loudly (varying the dynamics), fast passages slowly (varying the speed) or quick passages in dotted rhythms (varying the rhythm). The question is how best to do this. A teacher will help but, with limited lesson time, can't make every possible suggestion. The following ideas may provide a starting point. Ideas specifically for pianists are given in **Practising for pianists** on page 66.

Warm ups

- ❑ For teenagers and adults (not usually necessary for young children), I recommend a few minutes of physical warm-ups before starting music practice. These will get the blood circulating, stimulate the brain and relax the body, thus making the practice more effective. Pick your favourite exercises (of the swinging arms and rolling shoulders variety) from an expert such as Penelope Roskell on her *Yoga for Musicians* DVD[26].

- ❑ Always get ready to play with good posture and soft relaxed arms and hands and, for wind players, embouchure.

- ❑ Start your practice with exercises, scales and arpeggios and/or studies in order to warm up your fingers and to prepare physically and mentally – it takes a while to build the focus and concentration to listen carefully.

- ❑ Develop the ability to listen carefully – to hear what you are playing. Little useful practice can be achieved without listening acutely to elements such as the quality of sound, the articulation and the dynamics.

Accuracy

- ❑ Stop at each mistake and practise the difficulty, otherwise you may not remember them – don't fudge – all the notes are important.

- ❑ Practise a beat or a bar up to speed and stop, play the next beat or bar and stop – at each stop review what you have done and think about what you want to do next – listen, look and analyse.

- After attempting a difficult passage several times and finally playing it successfully, it is important to repeat the passage correctly several times, otherwise the incorrect one which has been played many times will be retained better than the correct one which has been played only once.

- Set the metronome to a comfortable speed and play the complete piece in strict time. Note the places where your technique struggles to keep up, and practise those passages. When you have a good understanding and control of the steady pulse, you can vary the pulse, eg slowing down at the ends of phrases.

- Alternate playing with the metronome and without it in order to retain your own sense of pulse.

- Learn to play the piece faster than necessary so the final speed can sound and feel easy.

- For string players, it is essential to separate right hand from left hand practice – bowing patterns and string crossing need to be worked on separately from fingerwork and shifting.

- For pianists, hands separate practice is essential (see ***Practising for pianists : Separate hands*** on page 67).

- For a young child, playing a short section 'perfectly' twice may be sufficient challenge for one practice.

Security

- Memorise awkward page turns.

- Memorise difficult sections.

- Memorise the whole piece.

- Mime a passage from memory.

- Play with your eyes closed.

Tackling problems

- Temporarily allow yourself to play inaccurately – wrong notes, loose rhythm, poor intonation. First practise the movements, the feel, the sound – even deliberately playing wrongly. Use the whole body freely. Then gradually focus on one aspect at a time to improve it.

- Focus on the smallest issue – break up the problem into simple parts, eg identify scale and arpeggio patterns, awkward leaps, tricky rhythms, and practise short sections accordingly.

- Make the problem more complex, eg if there is a leap of one octave, practise leaping two, three and four octaves (if you can play that many octaves on your instrument); when you return to the actual interval it seems, in comparison, easier.

- Practise a tricky passage in different keys, in different rhythms, with your eyes shut.

- Practise tiring loud passages also softly to conserve your energy.

- Practise very soft passages also strongly so your fingers are energetic and don't get lazy.

❑ Practise the awkward passage, then also practise the lead into the passage to ensure you arrive at that awkward patch in a controlled fashion.

❑ Play an awkward passage four times perfectly at a slow metronome speed, increase the metronome incrementally, playing four times perfectly at each speed; next day start one metronome speed higher than where you started the previous day.

❑ Pianists work hands separately.

❑ String players practise left hand alone, but also don't neglect working on the subtleties of right arm bow technique.

❑ Wind players finger the passage without blowing.

❑ Start your practice with the most awkward part of a piece – while you are fresh and so it gets covered every day.

Awkward fingering

❑ If the fingering seems awkward, check to see if an alternative fingering might suit you better, playing the passage slowly and ignoring the rhythm at first. Repeat the passage until the fingers play correctly automatically.

❑ Practise the passage *staccato* as well as *legato*.

❑ Practise in different rhythms such as:

See also **Practising for pianists: Fingering** on page 69 and **Practising scales and arpeggios for pianists: Fingering** on page 77.

Complex rhythms

❑ Complex rhythms may be best learned away from an instrument by singing or by tapping the rhythm, sometimes using a metronome.

❑ Count slowly in the shortest rhythmic unit – not just counting but also feeling the pulse – lead in by counting two bars of, eg, semiquavers.

Evenness

❑ Practise in different rhythms such as:

❑ For even flow in semiquaver passages, practise detaching slightly after the first note of each group (or after the second or third note) while maintaining the correct tempo:

❑ Practise with stops – wait and relax on the first beat of the bar, play the bar up to speed and wait and relax on the first beat of the next bar, and so on.

❑ Practise *staccato*, double *staccato* (each note twice) and triple *staccato* (each note three times).

Mosaic practice

- ❑ Work at all similar passages in the piece, eg melody throughout, accompaniment throughout, all *staccato* sections, all *piano* sections, all semiquaver passages.

- ❑ Choose a piece with stepped dynamics, eg *piano* and *forte* but not *diminuendo* and *crescendo*. First play all the soft parts, then all the strong ones – exaggerate how soft and how strong. Then play from the beginning of the piece, stopping at each change of dynamic, ie play *forte* section – stop – play *piano* section – stop – play *forte* section – stop – and so on. Again, exaggerate the contrasts. Then play straight through the piece with no stops, being very aware of the dynamics and exaggerating them.

Opposites

- ❑ Practise opposites, eg upwards scale downwards, grace note C-B also B-C, *legato* passages *staccato* and double *staccato*.

- ❑ Deliberately practise exaggerating the opposite of what you want. For example, upbeats generally need to be played softly. Try playing the upbeat *too* softly – question how it feels, how it sounds. Then play the upbeat strongly – again, how does it feel, how does it sound? Decide what sound you want – how it feels – listen to the sounds, and learn to control the sounds you really want.

- ❑ Sometimes practise slow pieces fast to understand the structure, phrasing, climax; practise fast pieces slowly to get the detail precise.

- ❑ Practise either playing from memory, or keeping your eyes on the music (without looking at your hands) – avoid constantly moving your eyes from your hands to the music.

Ornaments

- ❑ Be clear about how many and which notes are to be played.

- ❑ Practise the ornament slowly and softly and gradually speed it up, but keeping it soft.

- ❑ Isolate the ornament – omit the notes before or after or underneath. Mime the ornament on the key surface, hardly moving your fingers, or on the fingerboard with no bow on stringed instruments, or without blowing for wind instruments. Then do the opposite and practise lifting your fingers energetically and playing strongly, then back to miming – then play very softly.

- ❑ Practise the passage omitting ornaments, then add the ornaments as subtle decorations.

Repeats

- ❑ If there is a problem remembering repeats, try playing strongly the first time and softly on the repeat, or *vice versa*.

- ❑ If a repeat is forgotten, keep going, but then play the whole piece again afterwards.

- ❑ Listen to recordings of the piece so the structure is in your mind.

Repetition

- ❏ It is better to spend a few minutes on one awkward passage than play through a whole piece – work on the same short passage every day until it becomes easy.

- ❏ Practise a short section several times, stop, repeat it several more times. However, repetitions can be overdone – after a while the passage can get worse. Change to practising something else and return to the repetitions later, or at the following practice.

- ❏ Play a phrase several times, deliberately varying it each time, eg in different rhythms, articulation, dynamics, accenting different notes, playing at different octaves, or with different bowings or tonguings.

- ❏ Repeat short phrases for clarity, feeling the intervals, harmonies and rhythms.

- ❏ Some passages lend themselves to circular practice, in which a few notes or a bar can be played round and round in circles without stopping.

- ❏ Practise backwards – practise the last bar or phrase of a piece or section of a piece, then practise the last two bars or phrases, then the last three bars or phrases, and so on.

- ❏ Practise adding a note at a time – play the first two notes of a passage, ensuring you end cleanly on the final note, repeat twice correctly, then add another note, and so on.

- ❏ Don't practise your mistakes repeatedly – you may get very good at them.

- ❏ Repetition is the mother of tuition[27].

Slow motion practice

Benefits

- ❏ Practice slowly (half speed or even slower) to reveal any insecurities. Slow work is like using a magnifying glass – everything can be seen more clearly – it gets very interesting.

- ❏ Practise so slowly there are no wrong notes.

- ❏ Practise very softly and very slowly to develop appropriate refined movements.

- ❏ Practise very slowly to improve co-ordination, for control of fast notes, for clarity, so music doesn't sound rushed, to let music breathe.

- ❏ It is not difficult to play quickly if everything can be played very well slowly.

- ❏ Practise slowly to listen for a beautiful sound on every note and enjoy the harmonies.

- ❏ Slow practice can be relaxing and therapeutic.

Exercises

- ❏ Every day practise a short section (eg a page, or two lines) very slowly.

- ❏ Take one piece and, for a whole week, practise it *only* very slowly – at the end of the week play it up to speed and marvel at the improvement.

Practice techniques

- ❏ When practising slowly, exaggerate everything, eg dynamics, articulation – it is easy to play everything a uniform medium loudness, and to play long staccato notes instead of short, crisp ones. Exaggerate the contrasts.

- ❑ Turn scale passages into beautiful melodies – feel physical pleasure while practising them slowly.

- ❑ When practising slowly, move fast to prepare for the next note.

- ❑ Practise slowly with the metronome set to the quaver or semiquaver pulse to improve uneven rhythm.

- ❑ Practise with the metronome set to a slow speed (pianists – first each hand separately, then hands together); when perfect increase the metronome speed.

- ❑ If there is a tendency to rush – think of the character of the piece, think of getting slower, or play with the metronome, or with a recording, or parent/teacher play one hand while pupil plays other.

- ❑ Alternate slow practice with fast practice – after practising something slowly, play it up to speed to feel the actual movements required.

Anecdotes

- ❑ Practise fast, progress slowly; practise slowly, progress fast.

- ❑ The faster the piece, the slower the practice.

- ❑ The cleverer you are, the slower you can play.

- ❑ One of the finest concert pianists ever, Rubinstein, played his concert pieces very slowly on the day of a concert. Every day he practised a little very slowly.

- ❑ Another outstanding concert pianist, Richter, was said to practise so slowly one could not tell what piece he was playing.

Tips and Tricks

"Any mistake, or less than acceptable result, made within a passage is more than likely to repeat itself unless corrective action is taken", writes double bassist Duncan McTier[28]. **"Faults do not correct themselves merely by repetition!** Before a passage can be improved, the player must first play detective, analyse the result of the previous attempt, and decide on what plan of action is required ... to improve it. Particularly in the early stages of working on a piece, there are likely to be numerous imperfections, all of which will require a corrective thought [and action]. It is imperative to work slowly enough, or on sections that are sufficiently small, for the player to be able to notice ... all the problems. The better trained the memory, and the fewer the imperfections, the larger the section of music that can be practised productively."

Chapter 6: Learning new pieces

It is always exciting to start a new piece. While your enthusiasm is high, it is important to get off to a good start in order to gain the most benefit from your enthusiasm. Your teacher may have played the piece to you in the lesson. You may already have heard the piece and asked to learn it. There may be recordings of the piece – if so, listen to as many different recordings as possible in order to hear several different interpretations. Good role models are invaluable.

Plan of work

- ❑ When starting a new piece, first play it through to get an overview of the whole work. Identify the form (eg binary, ternary, rondo, sonata form – see *Glossary* on page 97 for definitions); look at the shape (eg dynamic, harmonic, rhythmic, melodic) of each section. Play the scale and arpeggio of the key of the piece.

See *Analysis of folk song: Go tell Aunt Rhody* on page 91.

- ❑ Divide the music into sections for practice, according to the structure of the music – the more complex the music, the shorter the sections.

- ❑ As practice progresses, the sections will become longer.

- ❑ The more difficult the music, especially if rhythmically, harmonically or melodically complex, the more it may be necessary to study the music away from the instrument.

Learning the notes

- ❑ Work on a short section at a time – for beginners this may be only two or three notes. Repeat until they are perfect several times consecutively, each time listening carefully for further improvements in rhythm, articulation, intonation, dynamics, and so on. Add another note or two. Repeat until perfect several times (pianists probably hands separately). If there is a particular problem, analyse it, reduce it to its simplest, and devise an exercise to overcome it. This is a much more efficient way of learning than playing through the whole piece a few times.

- ❑ Check fingerings, bowings and articulation carefully.

- ❑ For pianists, it is useful to learn each hand separately to ensure technical security and musical understanding. Learn the left hand first to prevent it being neglected and because it usually provides the harmonic foundation, then learn the right hand.

- ❑ Work on technically demanding passages in short sections. When these are mastered, work on longer sections, then on the whole piece.

- ❑ Practise small blocks up to speed, then join blocks together.

- ❑ If you start by working on the most difficult bar, section or movement, and then progress forwards and backwards from those awkward bits – putting them into context – gradually the whole piece will be mastered at the same time.

- ❑ To learn the notes of difficult passages, simplify by removing the rhythm or the articulation or the ornamentation – reduce the passage to its bare basics before building it up again.

Developing fluency

❏ Stop before an awkward note or finger change to prepare mentally and physically; repeat several times; gradually you will be able to play it fluently without a stop.

❏ When the piece is nearly mastered, play it from the beginning until there is a wrong note/finger/rhythm. Practise the two or three awkward notes until perfect several times. Then start a bar before the awkward patch and practise the two bars until perfect several times. Then start earlier – at the beginning of the phrase or section – and repeat until perfect several times.

❏ Focus on one point at a time. If you are trying to improve three things, eg smoother right hand melody, softer left hand accompaniment, and more varied dynamics, work on one point, then on the second, then on the third – the result with be more successful than initially working on all three points together.

❏ When the notes have been learnt but the piece is not yet fluent, set a slow metronome and repeat until perfect at that speed (pianists hands separately and then together), which may take several days. When perfect, increase the speed of the metronome by one notch, and repeat until perfect – again, it may take several days. When perfect, increase the metronome speed. By now it will probably not take long to play the piece perfectly, and then increase the speed.

❏ If speed is really an issue, build up the speed until you are playing as fast as is comfortable with the metronome set to the crotchet pulse. Then set the metronome to a minim pulse – and you may find you can now play it faster. Now play feeling one beat in a bar, and even feeling one beat every two bars.

Playing musically

Sound

❏ Always listen for beautiful sounds.

❏ Sometimes practise very softly, but still with good quality sound.

❏ Project the melody even when it is marked soft.

❏ Let the music breathe before the first beat.

❏ Take care with repeated notes – don't clip the first note.

❏ Orchestrate your sounds – imagine different instruments and different colours.

Phrasing

❏ Shape the phrases well, eg according to the harmonies, or feeling a question and answer.

❏ Often phrases are rainbow shaped – starting softly, rising in tone, then ending softly.

❏ Lift/breathe at the end of one phrase before beginning the next.

❏ To feel phrases naturally, sing the piece in your head and out loud before playing it.

❏ If your pulse varies, practise conducting the piece while someone else plays it, or conduct a recording of the piece.

Rhythm

- ❑ Playing with the correct rhythm and maintaining the pulse is usually more important than playing all the correct notes.

- ❑ Keep dotted rhythms very crisp – don't degenerate into triplets:

 not

- ❑ Generally, play shorter notes softer than longer ones.

- ❑ Upbeats are usually lighter – but nurture them – play with good quality sound.

Dynamics

- ❑ Exaggerate dynamic contrasts.

- ❑ Generally start a *crescendo* quietly, and start a *diminuendo* loudly.

- ❑ When a *crescendo* is followed by *subito piano*, place the first soft note – delay playing it.

- ❑ Imagine *pp* (*pianissimo* – very soft) = play positively or project positively.

- ❑ Keep the notes before and after a *sforzando* (accent) very soft for maximum contrast.

Interpretation

- ❑ Grasp the mood of each piece.

- ❑ Use gesture as a means of bringing the character, drama and rhythm into focus – breathe with the music.

- ❑ To decide the speed, play the most difficult passage, or sing the melody.

- ❑ Dramatic rests and pauses – wait over the notes – listen to the silences – don't move until the last moment to prepare for the next note.

- ❑ Take risks.

- ❑ Practise spontaneity!

Mental rehearsal

- ❑ Listen to your piece in your head, or listen to a recording, either following the score or from memory.

- ❑ Listen to your piece (in your head, or to a recording), meanwhile silently practising (miming) the fingering.

- ❑ Listen to your piece in your head, studying the score and imagining the sounds and dynamics – orchestrate the sounds.

- ❑ Listen to many different recordings of your piece, sometimes following the score. Decide what you like most about each recording, and what you would do differently.

- ❑ Analyse the piece – ask yourself why the composer chose those notes, and what are the underlying harmonies.

- ❑ Study original editions of the music.

How to practise two specific pieces
Minuet in G for piano by Christian Petzold (1677-1733)

Minuet in G

Petzold

I have chosen a simple piece for this example with the intention that it can be understood even by those with little knowledge of music, and that the principles of practice can be transferred to more complicated music. In most respects, however advanced the music, these same principles of practice apply: analyse the piece, divide it into sections for practice, work at short sections – slowly, hands separately, memorising as you go, breaking down and repeating awkward passages – then gradually rebuild it into longer sections.

Practice	RH = right hand LH = left hand	**Principle**
Preparation This is a well-known minuet, once attributed to JS Bach, from the Baroque period when much music was based on the dance. Prominent composers of this period include Bach, Handel and Vivaldi. You might like to listen to a recording of this minuet or other minuets by Baroque composers. Imagine elegant ladies and gentlemen in elaborate clothes. The dancing would be very stately! An exquisite performance of this piece, together with expert advice		*Listen to recording to feel the style*

on interpreting and practising music by Bach, is given by Angela Hewitt on her DVD *Bach Performance on the Piano*[29].

Sight read complete piece – hands together if possible, otherwise hands separately, after playing the scale and arpeggio of the key of the piece: G major.

Note the piece is in triple time; it is a minuet (which always has three beats in a bar); it is a dance, so the 2nd and 3rd beats should sound lighter than the 1st.

Sight read piece and analyse it

Note the two sections A (bars 1-16) – repeat – B (bars 17-32) – repeat, ie binary form.

Note RH bars 1-6 and 9-14 are identical, while 7-8 and 15-16 are slightly different. LH bars 1-6 are similar to bars 9-14 but slightly varied.

Start working on one 8-bar section, eg bars 1-8, with each hand separately.

Divide piece into sections

Possible problems

Analyse problems

Chord in LH bar 1 (also RH bar 32)
All notes need to sound exactly together.
Practise each pair of notes of chord together 4x, then all three notes 4x.
Practise chord *staccato* 4x, then *legato* 4x.
Practise chord strongly 4x, then softly 4x.

Simplify
Vary articulation
Vary dynamics

Big interval, eg LH bar 8
Practise LH bar 8 repeatedly, looking at music, then at hands, then with eyes closed:

Repeat tricky passages, short at first, getting longer

Start from previous bar several times:

Finish phrase by repeating bars 7+8 plus 1st note of bar 9:

Start at bar 5 and play bar 5 through to 1st note of bar 9.
Play from the beginning through to bar 9 being aware of distances of big intervals.

Quavers need to sound even, eg RH bar 1
To develop control, practise up scale from G to D:

Vary repetitions:

    slowly, lifting fingers well and gripping strongly
    staccato
    double *staccato* (each note twice)
    legato in different rhythms such as:

Practise slowly
Vary articulation

Vary dynamics

with different dynamics, eg strongly, softly, starting soft
and getting louder, starting loud and getting softer.

Awkward leap, eg RH bars 2-3

Practise repeatedly leap from finger 2 on G to 3 on E – let arm circle
round, making a rainbow shape in the air.
Practise all bar 2 to 1st note of bar 3:

*Repeat
awkward leap
– isolate it,
then put it into
context*

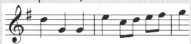

Add another bar – practise bars 2-3 and 1st note of bar 4 (listening for
even quavers):

Play bars 1-4 being aware of hand movement for leaps.
Ditto LH bars 12-13 – awkward fingering – 4 on G to 1 on A:

*Repeat
awkward
fingering*

Memorise bars 1-8 hands separately

Memorise

Then learn (and memorise) bars 9-16 hands separately.
At this stage you can decide to continue either by learning bars 17-24
followed by 25-32 hands separately, or to put bars 1-8 (and 9-16)
hands together.

When putting piece hands together, repeat bars 1+2 several times
until comfortable. Then bars 3+4 should be relatively easy to put
together. Repeat bars 1-4 several times until they seem easy, then
work on bars 5+6 together, and onto bars 7+8.

*Put hands
together –
repeat short
sections*

If there is a tricky section to put hands together (eg bars 7-8), play
each hand separately several times, perhaps singing the other
hand(!), then try it very slowly hands together.
Or play just the 1st two notes together several times, the 1st three
notes, the 1st four notes, and so on. Repetition of what you can do
well is better than hacking through the whole piece poorly.

*Repeat tricky
sections hands
separately
and together
and slowly*

Other points to listen for

Other points

Overlapping notes in LH bars 25+26+29

Work carefully to ensure all the notes are held down as long as they
should be (ask your teacher if you are unsure of this!) – check the
score and your fingers with your eyes and check the sounds with
your ears.

*Look and
listen for
accuracy*

Scale passages, eg RH bars 21+29

Start softly and get louder to the top of the scale at the 1st beat of
the next bar.
Practise just the two scale passages, RH alone, then hands together,
then start each the bar before.

*Shape scale
passages*

Long crotchets, eg bars 22+23

These bars have only crotchets (no quavers) and there can be a tendency to rush them. Think of the speed of the quavers of the previous bar and feel two quavers as you play each crotchet – deliberately try to slow down and you will probably play at the correct speed.

Feel pulse in shortest note values

Final chord – top note G needs to sing

Play RH bars 29-32 but ending F$^{\#}$-G (no chord) so you can hear how the tune needs to sound.

Practise playing the final G strongly on its own and then, while holding the G, softly play together the B and D of the chord. Then reverse – 1st play the B and D softly, then strongly play the G over the top. Play the B and D from the key surface for a softer sound, lift the finger and grip more for the G for a stronger sound. Lean the hand towards the fifth finger for the stronger G.

Separate different elements

When the piece is nearly learned, play through in longer sections, eg repeat the A section (bars 1-16) several times, each time listening for quality of sound, good balance between the hands, musical shaping of the phrases, accurate rhythms and a dance-like feel. Then do the same with the B section (bars 17-32).

Polish in longer sections

Typical features of this minuet which occur in much music of the Baroque period (c1600-1750)

Crotchet followed by four quavers, eg bars 1+3:

Sing strongly on longer note (crotchet), play softer on shorter notes (quavers).

Sing on 1st beat of bar, softer on 2nd and 3rd beats.

Start 2nd beat quavers softly and grow up scale to 1st note of next bar.

Three crotchets – um cha cha, eg RH bars 2 and 4:

Sing on high note – 1st beat of bar.

Play soft, light and short on low notes – 2nd and 3rd beats of bar.

LH minim tonic – down 8ve tonic, eg bar 16, and
LH three crotchets tonic – dominant – tonic, eg bar 32:

Sing on 1st beat, get softer through bar.

Relax hand on each note – don't remain stretched out.

Contrapuntal music – music written with two equally important parts

Play with a good strong tone in each hand (it is not a strong melody with a soft accompaniment). Imagine the RH and the LH being played by a violin and a cello, or an oboe and a bassoon – two equally important instruments.

Waltz in G Op39 No15 for violin by Johannes Brahms (1833-1897)

Practice

Preparation

This piece is a lovely example of romantic style and a good opportunity to learn to play expressively. It needs fluent, flexible playing all through the bow, and if you already do vibrato that is an asset. If you can listen to a recording (either of the original piano duet, or Brahms's own arrangement for piano solo, or this violin arrangement), it will help you absorb the sound and style. You can follow the music while you listen, or if you like moving to music, then find out in what ways it makes you want to move – smooth and gliding, or jumpy? The waltz is a dance particularly connected with Brahms' home city of Vienna. Listen to other waltzes (eg by Strauss or Tchaikovsky), or try dancing one yourself!

First stage

Think about the key. Play G major scale and arpeggio two octaves. Play musically and with an expressive sound and you will already be working on the style of the piece.
Try playing the whole piece through to get the feel of it.

Structure

Notice the structure of the whole piece. There are two sections, each with 1st and 2nd time endings. In addition, the 1st part is repeated halfway through the 2nd section, with a different ending (compare bar 21 with bar 7) to take the music back to G major instead of into B minor, as at the end of the 1st section. So the form is A A B A B A, with A being bars 1-8 and B bars 9-15.

Principle

Listen to recording to feel the style

Play scale and arpeggio of key of piece
Play complete piece

Analyse structure and shape

Technical problems

Bow control

You need good control of your bow speed as there are generally two beats in the down-bow and only one beat in the up-bow. Practise on the open A, minim then crotchet, listening for legato bowing without any bumps. You'll probably find that the up-bow sticks out like a sore thumb to start with! Practise going deeper into the string on the down-bow, and lightening the pressure on the up-bow until you can do it smoothly. It's rather like rowing a boat – the oars go in deeply to send the boat forward, then skim back over the surface. Or you can imagine your down-bow is moving through thick treacle, and your up-bow sliding on ice. Once you've mastered this bowing on one note, practise the 1st bar carefully. Make sure the string-crossing to the D-string is legato, and listen for good tone on the D-string. You need a flexible bow-hand and bow-arm to find the wavy feeling you need for this. Once you can do this bar well, then you are set up for the rest of the piece.

Practise bow control with different bow speeds

Technique for sound on ornament

To keep your fingers light for the grace notes such as in bar 3, think of 'pecking' the string with your 3rd finger. Keep the bow well into the string so the sound of the little notes is clear. Make sure bow and 1st finger are co-ordinated on the 2nd beat.

Play into string for clarity on ornament

String changing

At the end of bar 4 you need to glide your 3rd finger across from the D-string to the A-string without disturbing the legato. Try not to let it collapse on the A-string, which won't give you such good quality sound.

Glide finger across strings – keep a good finger position on A-string

Dynamics

By now you may have some sense of the rise and fall of this piece, which is rather like waves. Your dynamics should generally follow the shape of the phrases. Look especially at the B section from bars 9-15 – you can think of this as a hill with the highest note, A, at the top of the hill. You might like to highlight that note in your music. Now you are comfortable with the basic slow/quick bowing pattern, you can gradually use more bow to create an exciting crescendo up to the top of the hill, making sure you start softly with less bow at the bottom of the hill.

Shape phrases

The last phrase is the softest – imagine singing a baby or teddy-bear to sleep, or make up your own story-line to help play a beautiful ending to this piece. You could also experiment with using a point of contact for the bow which is slightly nearer the fingerboard when marked *p* to create a floaty sound, and nearer the bridge when *f* to achieve a more intense tone. Make sure, though, that you don't lose your singing sound.

Other points on style

Length of staccato

Decide just how short you want to play the two up-bow crotchets marked both *staccato* and *tenuto*, eg in bar 3. This is a question of personal taste, but the notes should have musical character and sound like part of the phrase, not like two up-bows.

Rubato

As you become more familiar with the piece, you will be able to let go into the one-in-a-bar feel of the rhythm. Then it will begin to flow more, and you can even introduce some *rubato*. This is not a piece to be too strict with the rhythm, once you know it well. For instance, take time around the corners, and you could linger on the last high A for as long as you dare!

Vibrato

If you do *vibrato*, use it to colour special notes, for instance that high A in bar 13.

Major/minor

Listen for minor tonality in the accompaniment from bars 5-8, and let it influence your sound and expression.

Expression

Lastly, always listen for warmth in the sound. Brahms' music is expressive and you need to wear your heart on your sleeve to play it!

Other points

Add character through length of staccato

Play freely with rubato

Use vibrato to colour special notes

Change quality of sound according to tonality

Play Brahms expressively

Chapter 7: Practising for pianists

As so many musicians play the piano in addition to an orchestral instrument, I feel it is appropriate to include a chapter specific to the piano. Many of these ideas can be adapted to other instruments.

Positive start

❏ Take a positive stance at the piano – sit tall, with your feet firmly placed on the floor (or on a footstool if you are still small), your shoulders and elbows relaxed, your lower arms roughly horizontal when playing – feel your confidence grow.

❏ Strive to make the piano a part of yourself – breathe with the music, think about your physical movements at the piano.

Warm ups

❏ Play a chord – sink in – feel flexible arms and strong fingertips – feel fluidity – play chords *very* slowly – feel the vibrations of each chord flow straight through you – listen to each chord – hear the sound going through the piano and back inside you – feel the piano is an extension of your hands – a sense of lifting the sounds up out of the piano rather than pushing the sounds in.

❏ Have strong, firm fingers, especially fingertips – imagine gripping onto a cliff edge, but with very light and loose wrists – play a few notes and stop to check flexibility – flexible, supple wrists produce a more beautiful tone.

❏ Play any big chord (major/minor/diminished) – feel very relaxed – circle wrists clockwise and anti-clockwise and up and down – then, while holding the chord, repeat any note with one finger four times (hands separately, then hands together).

❏ Repeat each chord three times – flex wrists before starting, wait after playing each chord, and listen to the quality of sound.

❏ Practise chords slowly with pedal – listen for pedal changes.

❏ Practise scales and arpeggios with one finger – just the fifth, or just the thumb – feel comfortable movements, listen for good quality sound.

Tone quality

❏ For a deep rich tone – play on the pad of the finger, squeeze, and roll onto the tip of the finger.

❏ For a deep sustained sound – transfer weight from finger to finger with no accents.

❏ For a smooth legato – imagine sticky glue on the tips of the fingers.

❏ Sustain the sound through repeated notes – don't allow the damper to touch the string, ie don't allow the key to come up completely before replaying.

❏ Listen for singing *legato* sounds – first without the pedal, then with the pedal.

❏ For colourful playing – vary the touch – fully bed the keys, or play half way down, or a quarter; or add arm weight – use your elbows.

❏ For sound production, to develop aural awareness – don't look at your hands – just feel and listen.

❏ The note after a long note (or a tied note) is generally soft (unless it is a new beginning) – the sound of the previous note has died.

Separate hands

Benefits

❏ Practise hands separately to develop control, and to improve technique, fluency, security and musical awareness.

❏ Practise hands separately to develop contrasting sounds in each voice of the music (eg the melody needs to sing out while the accompaniment needs to be soft, yet well-shaped).

❏ Be able to play each hand separately of a piece so if, in performance, one hand goes adrift, the other hand can continue until the first hand finds itself – neither hand should be dependent on the other.

❏ Memorise hands separately as well as together for extra security.

❏ Even after a piece is memorised, hands separate practice is as beneficial as hands together practice.

Exercises

❏ Practise the left hand alone, then hands together focusing on the left hand – listening to the left hand, watching the left hand, just miming the right hand or playing it very softly. Then *vice versa* – practise the right hand alone, then hands together focusing on the right hand.

❏ When practising separately, start with the left hand followed by the right hand so the left hand is not neglected.

❏ If there is a problem in one hand, eg fingering, lengths of notes or rests, dynamics, articulation, practise that hand *alone* and repeat it several times before playing it hands together again.

❏ Alternate practising a passage in the left hand with a passage in the right hand so neither hand gets over-tired.

❏ Practise soft left hand accompaniments strongly at first as well as softly to develop control and awareness in the fingers.

❏ Practise the left hand alone to be aware of it and to become fond of it.

❏ In complicated music, decide whether you need to look at the music, the right hand or the left hand – you can't look at all three, ie complicated music needs to be memorised.

❏ One practice a week – practise hands separately *only*, no hands together work.

❏ Take one piece and, for a whole week, practise it hands separately *only* – then listen to the improvement when it is next played hands together.

Challenges

- ❏ Be able to play each hand separately with eyes closed.
- ❏ Play the notes of one hand with the other hand (hands separately, then hands together!).
- ❏ Play one hand and mime the other – from memory!
- ❏ Play one hand and sing the other.
- ❏ For security, learn to play awkward passagework from memory with one finger only.

Balance

- ❏ Practise hands separately – learn to play the melody with a big singing tone (lifting the fingers well and squeezing with the fingertips) and the accompaniment with a gentle sound (keeping the fingers near the keys). Shape the harmonies as well as the melodic line.
- ❏ The bass is often the most important line after the melody – listen from the bottom up rather than the top down.
- ❏ In order to change the colour it is sometimes necessary to bring out bottom or inner parts rather than the top line.
- ❏ Mime the accompaniment on its own; then mime the accompaniment while playing the melody strongly; then allow a few accompaniment notes to sound while playing the melody; then aim for an appropriate balance.
- ❏ Play hands together looking *only* at the right hand, or *only* at the left hand, or with your eyes closed – listening very carefully to the balance.
- ❏ Hold a heavy book in the hand that plays the melody and a light book in the hand that plays the accompaniment to feel the difference required in the sound.
- ❏ Play a summary or harmonic skeleton – play an outline of the melody and bass together, omitting unnecessary details.

Voicing

- ❏ In contrapuntal music, practise each voice (bottom, middle, top) on its own, shaping it musically.
- ❏ Play any two out of three (or four) voices, or any three out of four voices.
- ❏ Play two voices in two separate hands.
- ❏ Sing one voice and play all the rest.
- ❏ Play one voice strongly and mime the other(s).
- ❏ Try bringing out each voice as a solo in order to hear and shape each line musically.
- ❏ Practise chord sequences emphasising different notes in turn – all the top notes, middle notes or bottom notes.

Fingering

- ❑ Use appropriate fingers to enhance the texture of the music and to suit the hand, generally avoiding too many hand position changes.

- ❑ Chopin identified the thumb as the centre of the hand – it can be very flexible, and it is easy to pivot on the thumb.

- ❑ Practise awkward passages *legato* (even if marked *staccato*) to work out fingering; then practise the passage *staccato* and double *staccato* (each note twice) for security.

- ❑ Practise the fingering without making any sounds – mime the passage.

- ❑ Practise with your eyes shut to develop security in your fingering.

Passagework

- ❑ For complicated figuration (fast runs) – work out the fingering and hand shapes – play up to a change of finger with a new hand position, then practise up to the next hand position change, ie divide quick passages into short groups of notes.

- ❑ Mime fast passages *non legato* on the surface of the keys – then sound the notes.

- ❑ For fast light passages – practise bedding the keys, then depressing the key half way, then only a quarter down.

- ❑ For lightness – imagine wearing long sleeves and holding onto the top of your sleeve – if you let go, your arm would drop; or play silently on top of the keys, then play very lightly.

- ❑ Practise *staccato*, double *staccato* and triple *staccato* on each note.

- ❑ Practise in different rhythms such as:

- ❑ Practise accenting different notes:

- ❑ At speed, it may be appropriate not to put the thumb under for extended arpeggio passages – just to move the whole hand.

Octaves

- ❑ Practise hands separately, slowly, and softly, relaxing the hand and arm between each octave, gradually building up speed and volume.

- ❑ If an octave is too much of a stretch, start by practising sixths.

- ❑ Play from the wrist – keep loose and relaxed – if possible, stay near the bottom of the black notes – no accents, no weight.

- ❑ Practise a passage with each octave once, then repeating each octave twice, then three times.

- ❑ Practise just the thumbs, or just the fifth finger.

❑ Choreograph octaves – make a shape with the hand and wrist to serve best the articulation.

❑ Usually play the top notes of octaves stronger; on a repeat it may be appropriate to provide variety by voicing the lower notes.

Block chords

❑ Play each note, then pairs of notes, in the chord double *staccato*, gripping well with the fingertips, feeling the weight of the keys beneath the fingers.

❑ Form the shape of the chord with the hand before dropping into the keys – see and hear the voicing in advance – imagine dropping into soft putty or damp sand.

❑ Voice chords – often it is appropriate to emphasise the top note. Play the lower notes softly, keeping your fingers close to the keys; then, holding the lower notes, play the top note strongly, stretching the finger and gripping, leaning the hand to that side. Or *vice versa*, first play the top note strongly, followed by playing the lower notes softly.

❑ Practise chords at all octaves up and down the piano, lifting the wrist – like a trampoline.

❑ Learn awkward chords by listening – playing them slowly, listening to the sounds, and to the harmonies, meanwhile ensuring you are playing with the correct fingering and articulation.

Arpeggiated chords

❑ Work out which note should be the strongest, and which notes are lighter.

❑ Practise the notes of the chord in different orders, not just bottom up or top down.

❑ Arpeggiate the chord slowly and softly; then repeat the arpeggiated chord several times, gradually getting faster.

Broken chord accompaniments

❑ Practise broken chords as solid chords – for learning notes, hand shapes and movements, and for memorising chord sequences.

❑ In four-time Alberti bass accompaniments play strong-soft-medium-soft and in three-time accompaniments play strong-soft-soft to give the rhythmic pulse.

❑ Practise playing the first bass note with a deep sound, waiting, then playing the remainder of the broken chord softly and lightly, keeping the fingers close to the keys:

❑ Practise stopping on any one of each of the four (or three) notes.

❏ First play just the lowest (bass) notes of each broken chord with a deep sound; then play only the remainder of each chord very softly:

❏ For practice, emphasise any one note of each four (or three) note pattern:

Leaps

❏ Move the hand in circles (or arcs or rainbows) rather than straight lines.

❏ Increase the size of the interval, eg practise the one octave leap, then increase it to two octaves, three octaves, etc; then when you return to the actual interval it seems, in comparison, easier.

❏ Play the first note or chord, move quickly to the new position and wait with a balanced hand (it is not necessary to play the second note/chord); then do the reverse – play the first note/chord as you wish it to sound, release the note/chord and wait with a relaxed hand hovering above that note/chord, then quickly move and play the second note/chord.

❏ Um-cha-cha bass – play the passage very slowly, but move your hand to the new position very fast, waiting in a balanced position over the note or chord to be played.

Trills

❏ Hold one note and repeat the other quickly.

❏ Double trill – hold two notes and trill the others.

Rests

❏ Keep your hands over the keys during rests – the music dies if you relax your hands onto your lap.

Pedalling

❏ Syncopated pedalling (the most commonly required form of pedalling) – play a scale with one finger, counting three slow beats on each note as follows: 1) play a note with your finger, 2) depress the pedal with your foot, 3) lift your finger, 1) lift your foot at the exact moment you play the next note of the scale. Listen for clean sounds when changing from one note to the next.

❏ Direct pedalling – play a sequence of detached triads – for each chord play with the fingers and depress the pedal at exactly the same time, then lift the fingers and the foot at the same time.

❑ Practise a piece hands separately with no pedal, then hands separately (especially left hand) with pedal, then hands together with no pedal, and finally hands together with pedal, listening carefully to the different results.

General

❑ Experiment by playing with total correctness (eg fussy articulation), then contrast it by playing with long phrases and lots of pedal, then chose a musically stylistic interpretation between the two.

❑ Lean forward into the piano for *fortes* and away for *pianos*; or it may be appropriate to lean forward for soft passages and sit back for huge chords; delay *sforzandos*; open your shoulders for a *crescendo*.

❑ Conduct recordings or sing the music and wave your hands around – for a sense of rhythm.

❑ Play your left hand and conduct with your right hand – do it logically following the phrase structure and climaxes.

❑ Play the bass and sing the melody to get a natural flow – you need space to breathe, eg it takes time to sing a wide interval such as a sixth.

❑ Avoid playing in a blank mode of interpretation – have an extra-pianistic sound in your head – orchestrate the sounds – have a colour and dynamic in mind.

Chapter 8: Building repertoire

One reason for building a repertoire of familiar pieces is to enhance the sense of achievement and the satisfaction of being able to sit down anytime, anywhere, and play favourite pieces, ideally from memory. Another reason for revising well-known pieces is to develop technical and musical skills. The better you play your repertoire pieces, the better you will play your newest pieces (and the faster you will learn them), because you have a secure bank of skills on which to draw. In this way only a few new techniques need to be learned to master each new piece. Daily review of repertoire pieces helps lengthen concentration span, improve self-confidence and, if not using the music, extend memory.

Increasing repertoire

- ❏ When you can perform one piece satisfactorily and are given a new piece, don't drop the first but practise the old and the new ones at the same time.

- ❏ Add a piece each month (or week, or term) to your repertoire.

Improving repertoire

- ❏ Concentrate on improving a particular aspect when reviewing, eg tone, intonation, rhythm, dynamics, phrasing, character, bowing, breathing, posture.

- ❏ Repertoire pieces should be practised hands separately (pianists), sometimes very slowly, and short difficult sections practised as necessary so that, in the lesson, your teacher can work on creating a truly musical performance.

- ❏ Practise sometimes with a metronome so you know what is the strict pulse. Then you can play the piece musically, eg lingering over ends of phrases, without the metronome.

- ❏ Listen to several recordings of a piece, play or mime along with each recording, then play solo.

- ❏ Thinking about the character and meaning of the music can improve the playing.

Maintaining repertoire

- ❏ To keep a piece fresh, sometimes play it only hands separately (pianists), plus practise awkward passages in different ways, eg with different rhythms, bowings, articulation or breathing, without playing through the whole piece.

- ❏ If a piece is forgotten, try listening to a recording of it several times.

- ❏ Keep records of progress when reviewing repertoire, eg a tick chart, as a recognition of accomplishments. The authority rests with the chart – whatever the chart shows must be played.

Chapter 9: Mastering scales and arpeggios

The ability to play scales and arpeggios well is fundamental to developing a good technique, including balanced hand and body position, control of bowing and breathing, fingering, articulation, dynamic control, fluency and stamina. A secure knowledge of scales and arpeggios will speed up the learning of new pieces, which are often based on scale and arpeggio patterns. A firm knowledge and understanding of different keys and the geography of the instrument will improve the ability to read at sight. How scales and arpeggios are practised is more important than what is practised.

Pattern of scales – circle of fifths

C major scale has no sharps or flats. On the piano, playing all the white notes from one C to the next C gives one octave of C major scale. Each new scale starts five notes higher than the previous scale (**C-D-E-F-G**), and an extra sharp (usually a black note on the piano) is added to the scale (see chart of circle of fifths below). The new sharp is the penultimate note of the scale, so G major, with one sharp, ends **F#**-G rather than F-G. Continue up five notes **G-A-B-C-D**. D major has two sharps – **F#** and **C#** (it retains the **F#** of G major, and adds the new penultimate note – **C#**).

The relative minor scale starts three semitones below the major scale, eg **C-B-B♭-A**. The minor scale is related to the major in that it shares the same key signature (A minor, like C major, has no sharps or flats in the key signature), though there will be 'accidentals' – extra sharps or flats in the scale.

In the chart below, major scales are designated by a capital letter and minor by lower case, eg C = C major and a = A minor.

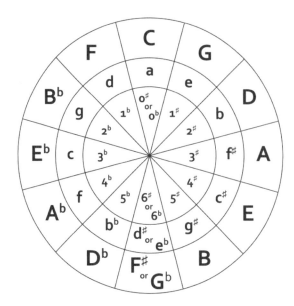

Purchase a good scale book, or ask a teacher, for details of notes and fingerings. Players of woodwind instruments, especially, need to understand the theory behind scales and arpeggios. Saying note names while miming fingerings helps memorise the patterns.

If you are still learning new scales, each week concentrate on one new scale, and revise the previous week's scale. If you have mastered all your scales, every day work on one scale in detail, then play one or more sets of twelve major, melodic minor or harmonic minor scales to develop familiarity.

For "scale", in this chapter, please read "scale or arpeggio".

Pianists: see also ***Practising scales and arpeggios for pianists*** on page 77.

Technique

- ❑ Start with fingers, hands and arms and, for wind players, embouchure in a relaxed position.

- ❑ Always listen carefully to the quality of sound.

- ❑ Play scales with different dynamics, eg *piano* or *forte*, *crescendo* or *diminuendo*.

- ❑ Play scales in different rhythms.

- ❑ Play scales with different articulation, bowing or breathing, eg *staccato* (each note once) or double *staccato* (each note twice).

- ❑ Feel the pulse on the first of each group of four notes (or, for practice, every two notes, three notes or five notes).

Knowledge of notes

- ❑ Practise by adding a note each time, ie play first note of scale, first two notes, first three notes, etc, each time using the correct fingers and accenting the last note:

- ❑ Practise scales with eyes closed.

- ❑ Play scales from bottom to top and down again, or from top to bottom and up again.

Familiarity

- ❑ Practise a scale one octave up and down until it is perfect. Then play the scale two octaves. If it is perfect, go on to playing it three octaves; if not perfect, go back to one octave. Continue until four octaves are perfect (if you can play four octaves on your instrument!).

- ❑ Set the metronome to 60. All at the same speed, without stopping, play a scale one octave up and down, then two octaves, three, four, three, two, and one octave (or as many octaves as can be played on your instrument).

❑ Play scales round the circle of fifths (see chart on opposite page) – all majors, then all melodic minors, then all harmonic minors. If one scale is not good, repeat it several times before going on to the next.

❑ Play the major scale followed by its relative minor round the circle of fifths.

❑ Play scales starting a semitone higher (or lower) each time (eg C, D^b, D, etc).

Speed

❑ Set the metronome to, eg, 60. Play one scale until it is perfect twice in a row. Increase the metronome speed to 63. Play the same scale again until it is perfect twice in a row. Increase the metronome to 66, etc.

❑ Set the metronome to 60. Play a scale:
- in crotchets, one octave, *forte*, using big movements/bow strokes/breaths
- in quavers, two octaves, *mezzo forte*, using smaller movements/bow strokes/breaths
- in triplets, three octaves, *mezzo piano*
- in semiquavers, four octaves, *piano* (if you can play four octaves on your instrument)
- in demisemiquavers, four octaves, *pianissimo*, using small movements/bow strokes/breaths!

❑ Practise just the top octave backwards and forwards for fluent change of direction.

Mental agility

❑ Play a scale one octave plus a note four times, then start on the second note of the scale up to the tenth note, etc.

❑ Play all twelve major/minor scales, but start each one on C (or C$^\#$ or C^b if no C in scale) – so that each scale has a completely different feel and sound.

❑ Teacher play a scale in contrary motion with a pupil, or in thirds; or one play *piano* and the other *forte*; one *crescendo* and the other *diminuendo*.

Chapter 10: Practising scales and arpeggios for pianists

Scales and arpeggios should be played beautifully, using the fingers well, listening for a deep, rich sound on each note. For faster scales, use smaller movements – lift the fingers less, but still squeeze with the fingertips. Don't push from the surface of the key as that produces a flat tone quality. Make the fingers dance. Treat scales artistically.

C major is the most difficult scale to play evenly and with the correct fingering; B major is the easiest because the pattern of black and white notes lies so well under the hands. Start learning B major, then F# major, then D♭ major, and so on round the circle of fifths (see chart on page 74). Initially study each scale one octave hands separately. If you are new to scales, each week work on a new scale, and also revise the previous week's scale. See also **Mastering scales and arpeggios** on page 74.

Fingering

- ❑ If there is a problem in one hand with the fingering, practise slowly just that hand separately, repeating one octave several times, then two octaves, three and four.

- ❑ If you know which note is played by the fourth finger in each hand, the other fingers will automatically play the correct notes.

- ❑ Stop on each tonic to check the fingering.

- ❑ Often there is more of a problem descending than ascending; often the left hand is less secure than the right hand; ie practise more the left hand alone descending.

Technique

- ❑ Practise very slowly in order to prepare the thumb under the hand and to listen for a smooth *legato*.

- ❑ Listen that the fourth finger (a weak finger) plays with a good tone.

- ❑ Practise loudly to develop strong fingers – play deep to the keybed, not on the surface – play with relaxed arms but strong fingers.

- ❑ Practise scales *staccato* to develop good fingertip movement – make the notes short and bouncy, but keep the hand close to the keys – let the fingers do the work – use a firm touch to produce a good sound.

- ❑ Practise with the left hand louder than the right hand to avoid the left hand getting lazy.

- ❑ Lean your body into the keyboard at the bottom and the top.

Sound

- ❑ Practise scales hands together, but also hands *separately*, listening carefully to every sound – in real music scales rarely appear hands together.

- ❑ Practise scales lightly using the soft pedal.

Familiarity

- ❑ Mime the right hand and play the left hand, then *vice versa*.
- ❑ Play hands together looking only at the left hand, then looking only at the right hand.
- ❑ Play scales using only one finger.

Speed

- ❑ Play a five-finger exercise – eg CDEFGFEDC – very slowly – lifting the fingers well – then play the same sequence of notes three times very fast, keeping the fingers close to the keys, and making circles with the wrist:

- ❑ Practise very fast but stop on every tonic – listen that the hands are exactly co-ordinated, especially on the last few notes before each tonic.

Mental agility

- ❑ Play one hand two octaves twice as fast as the other hand one octave.
- ❑ Play one hand three octaves in triplets against the other hand two octaves in duplets.
- ❑ Play scales two octaves apart.
- ❑ Play scales with crossed hands.
- ❑ Play scales with one hand *legato* and the other *staccato*, or one hand *piano* and one *forte* (alternating every four notes!).
- ❑ Play one hand two octaves up and down, and the other hand one octave up-down-up-down.
- ❑ Play scales in the 'Russian' way – two octaves up in similar motion, continue with two octaves in contrary motion, onwards with two octaves up and down in similar motion, two octaves in contrary motion, two octaves down in similar motion.

Technique for arpeggios

- ❑ Play an arpeggio with each hand separately one octave up and down several times, making the wrist circle round, using the full depth of the keyboard and relaxing the thumb under the hand.
- ❑ Play each note of the arpeggio double *staccato*, keeping your hand in a well balanced position – keep the thumb relaxed under the hand – first one octave, then two octaves.

Familiarity for arpeggios

- ❑ Play triads up and down the piano alternating right hand and left hand, eg first C major up and down the piano, then G major, D major, and so on, round the circle of fifths (see chart on page 74).

Also practise arpeggios in the ways suggested above for scales.

Chapter 11: Developing sight reading

It is possible that adult amateur musicians enjoy reading unseen music more than any other type of playing – it may be what they spend most of their time doing when they have a chance to play their instrument. They may be playing in an orchestra, in a small ensemble with friends, accompanying another instrumentalist, or playing duets. Adults enjoy being able to take their instrument and play through music 'at sight'. Those who can sight read fluently will be much quicker at learning new music than those who struggle to decipher notation.

Many children find sight reading difficult in the early stages, and cannot see a good reason for making an effort to develop this skill. If children can be convinced of the pleasures to be had, they may be more willing to spend the time practising reading. As with all skills, reading requires practice in order to become fluent. There is little evidence to suggest that talent has anything much to do with proficiency in sight reading[30]. Rather, it is a case of conscientious and creative practising. Also helpful is to become familiar with the style of the music being sight read – by listening to plenty of music as well as playing music in different styles.

Visual and aural reading skills

The early development of good reading ability requires progressive work on visual and aural reading skills. These skills may be developed in group lessons through games using flash cards to identify rhythms, pitches, musical terms, and so on, together with aural games and activity games, eg singing and clapping games.

- ❑ Using flash cards (or computer software programmes such as Hofnote[31] or CATS[32]), become familiar with the stave, clefs, space and line notes, pitches of notes and values of notes and rests.

- ❑ Start with the sound and progress to the visual – play C (perhaps A or D if you are a string player) and find it on a flash card.

- ❑ Play C (or A or D) from printed music and find more Cs (As, Ds) on the music. Play and draw Cs (As, Ds).

- ❑ When familiar with C, find a step up to D. Play the note, say its name, and find the card. Find the note on printed music and draw notes. When familiar, progress to E, then F and G.

- ❑ Learn to read by interval. Find intervals of a second (moving up or down by step) and a third (jumping line to line or space to space) – play them, name them, and identify the written notes.

- ❑ Challenge yourself to identify all the notes in the treble and bass clefs from flash cards in random order in one minute.

When you have developed good visual reading skills, as well as a good ear, physical co-ordination and mental concentration, you are ready for your first music reading book. When you are presented with your first reading piece, there should be nothing in the piece with which you are not familiar. Therefore, it will be easy for you and, therefore, you will be motivated to do more.

Reading music is very exciting. Practise reading every day. Play each reading piece several times, also hands separately (pianists), until you have mastered it. Be aware of the difference between 'prepared' reading (spending a day or a week on a quick study piece) and 'sight' reading (playing a piece once or twice and going on to the next one). It is important first to learn to *play* well, then to *read* well, then to *read at sight*. Prepared reading – repetition – is an important part of early reading practice. Each day, practise reading a new piece and then play through some reading pieces from the previous days' practices.

Prepare to read music

- ❏ Play one octave of the scale (and arpeggio) of the key of the piece.
- ❏ Tap the rhythm of the piece, tapping the pulse with the other hand.
- ❏ Name the notes.
- ❏ Identify the intervals.
- ❏ Hear the piece in your head.
- ❏ Sing it.
- ❏ Mime playing the piece.

Be a good detective

- ❏ Study the music carefully before playing it.
- ❏ Don't miss any clues – identify the key, time, clefs, dynamics, speeds, articulation, bowings, etc. From this examination, identify the character of the piece.
- ❏ Scan the music to identify scale passages, arpeggios, intervals, chords, accompaniment patterns, etc.
- ❏ Recognise groups of notes rather than reading notes singly.
- ❏ If rhythms are complicated, subdivide the beat, eg count four quavers in a bar rather than two crotchets.
- ❏ When the finger number is written on the music, it often signifies a change of hand position.

Read a piece

- ❏ Count a full bar before beginning.
- ❏ Always play in perfect time.
- ❏ Sometimes read with the metronome – rhythmic pulse and continuity distinguish good readers from bad.
- ❏ Keep your eyes on the music – if necessary, ask your teacher or parent to hold a sheet of paper over your hands to block out your view.
- ❏ Look ahead on the music – at least to the next beat or bar.

❑ Don't look back at what you have just played – occasionally ask your teacher or parent to cover up the music you have just played.

❑ Sit up straight – don't lean forward to peer at the music.

❑ Don't be too much of a perfectionist (save that for practising repertoire) – get the sense of the music.

Activities at instrument

❑ Look at one bar or phrase of music for ten seconds, cover it up and play it (to develop short-term memory).

❑ Transpose a sight reading piece.

❑ Improvise in the key of the piece (good improvisers tend to be good sight readers).

❑ Try playing the correct rhythm but improvising the notes (for perfectionists who will insist on going back to correct mistakes).

❑ The best sight readers don't look at their instrument while playing. Therefore, get used to playing your repertoire pieces without looking at your fingers, with your eyes closed, or in the dark.

Activities away from instrument

❑ Decide on the character of the piece simply by looking at the score. Look at the title (if any) of the piece. Look at the *tempo* marking (speed). Look especially at the articulation – long smooth phrases may indicate an unhurried, calm flowing piece; *staccato* dots may indicate a faster, lively piece. Look at the dynamics – establish the climax. Consider the shape – perhaps like a mountain – and draw it in the air. Build a picture in your mind.

❑ Make a list of all the musical terms and signs encountered in your pieces, and keep adding to the list.

Fun with reading

❑ Teacher and pupil read duets regularly in lessons – make music together for enjoyment.

❑ Teacher and pupil alternate playing a bar each; or one play all the naturals (white notes on the piano) and the other play sharps and flats (black notes) in the piece.

❑ Two pupils sight read duets in adjacent/overlapping lessons.

❑ Plan duets for pupils of similar age, or for younger pupils with older pupils.

❑ Encourage family duets or trios with siblings or parents.

❑ One pupil accompany another.

❑ Sight read double duets and trios in group lessons, ie four or six pupils together.

Music for reading

Many books are available for developing sight reading skills. Pupils need a variety of material, alternating between 'real' music (eg Bartok, Kabalevsky) and 'sight reading' pieces (eg Bullard,

Harris). Books with accompanying recordings are useful for developing the ability to keep going whether or not playing perfectly. Duets and other ensemble playing are much to be recommended for improving sight reading abilities.

List of music for sight reading

The following list may provide a starting point.

Piano solo

Carol Barratt	Sight-read with Chester	Chester Music
Carol Barratt	Piano Starters	Chester Music
Carol Barratt	Play it Again, Chester	Chester Music
Bela Bartok	Mikrokosmos	Boosey & Hawkes
Stephen Duro	Finger Jogging Boogie	ABRSM Publishing
Alan Bullard	Joining the Dots	ABRSM Publishing
Mark Goddard	Simplest Scottish Jigs and Reels	Spartan Press
Donald Gray (ed)	Very First Classics	Boosey & Hawkes
Paul Harris	Improve your Sight Reading	Faber Music
Thomas Johnson	Read and Play	Hinrichsen
Dmitri Kabalevsky	24 Little Pieces	Boosey & Hawkes
John Kember	Starting Out	Schott
Joan Last	Sight Reading for Today	Bosworth
Martha Mier	Jazz, Rags and Blues	Alfred Publishing
Elissa Milne	Little Peppers series	Faber Music
Christopher Norton	Microjazz series	Boosey & Hawkes
Ernest Van de Velde	Methode Rose	Editions Van de Velde
Fanny Waterman	Piano Playtime	Faber Music
Pamela Wedgwood	Upgrade	Faber Music
Pamela Wedgwood	After Hours	Faber Music

Piano duet

Waterman/Harewood	Two at the Piano	Faber Music
Waterman/Harewood	Me and My Piano	Faber Music
Barbara Kirkby-Mason	First Duet Album for Piano	Bosworth
Diabelli	Melodic Exercises Op149	Peters
Martha Mier	Jazz, Rags and Blues for Two	Alfred Publishing

Music for other instruments

Browse in a good music shop where the staff may be able to give helpful advice on available material.

Chapter 12: Getting motivated

Learning to play an instrument well is hard work. Keeping a student motivated is a challenge for teachers and parents alike. The hope is that, eventually, students will be motivated by the pleasure they derive from their achievements. However, in the early stages, students are likely to require motivation from external sources.

Stimulation

Goals

- ❑ Identify a short term goal for a specific problem.

- ❑ Practise to a target, eg lesson, ensemble rehearsal, concert, examination, audition, festival performance.

Performances

- ❑ Perform at pupils' concerts and festivals.

- ❑ Perform at school, college or church.

- ❑ Give a concert for parents, relatives, friends and neighbours.

- ❑ Give a fancy dress solo concert.

- ❑ Perform in places with good acoustics.

Listening

- ❑ Record and listen back to your own performance.

- ❑ Ask other members of your family to play music to you (if they can).

- ❑ Listen to plenty of music – recordings and live performances.

Playing for fun

- ❑ Play pop tunes, folk music, Christmas carols, etc.

- ❑ Play by ear.

- ❑ Improvise.

Practising

- ❑ Don't put your instrument away, then it's easier to fit in a short practice.

- ❑ Have a lucky dip with practice points – a box with each practice point written on a separate piece of paper or card – draw out the card and practise accordingly; also for daily review of scales and repertoire pieces.

- ❑ To prevent a piece getting stale, work only on short sections daily, but don't play the piece straight through. Then reward yourself by playing right through the piece at the end of your practice – this will reveal what needs most work next time.

Imagination

- ❑ It may not be fun to practise – it is hard work – then it becomes interesting.

❑ Use your imagination – find new ways of practising – don't practise in the same way every day.

Young children

Very young children may be practising with a parent, or at least a parent may be listening on the sidelines. Occasionally suggesting one of the following games may provide much needed motivation for your child. Even if, at that practice, less progress seems to be made on the work set by the teacher, the added interest will have far-reaching effects on your child's subsequent motivation to practise.

Games

❑ Name favourite and least favourite football teams. Child works on an assignment – if successful, favourite team scores; if not, other team scores.

❑ Repeat a tricky passage the number of times of your child's age – if it goes wrong, start counting again.

❑ Count down towards zero – this heightens concentration.

❑ Play the same short section sitting on every chair in every room in the house (difficult for pianists!).

❑ Try practising for a calculated number of minutes before a favourite television programme.

❑ Ask children to spend an equal number of minutes practising as they do playing on the computer!

Activities

❑ Make a jigsaw, colour a square, colour in a picture or do a dot-to-dot for every ten repetitions.

❑ Collect bricks to build a tower at the end of the practice.

❑ Put together pieces of a wooden toy or win a piece of lego for each repetition.

❑ Use an abacus to record the number of repetitions.

❑ Roll a dice to decide how many times to practise a certain passage.

❑ Use an egg timer.

Fun

❑ Sing silly words.

❑ Sing seriously.

❑ Parent play the piece badly and child teach the parent.

❑ Parent play the same hand as the child plays, then parent play the other hand from the child (pianists); or parent play accompaniment (to orchestral instrument).

❑ Parent play duets with child.

❑ For relaxation between pieces, shake like a wet dog.

Rewards

- ❑ Win a smartie or sticker for every ten correct repetitions.

- ❑ Write a practice assignment on an envelope – negotiate what goes into the envelope at the end of the week.

- ❑ Mummy give child a kiss for every repertoire piece played beautifully (or child give mummy a kiss!).

- ❑ Light a candle for the duration of each practice – a prize when the candle has burnt down.

- ❑ If the child argues with the parent about practice, the teacher could write the teaching point in the notebook with a box for a tick for each day's practice. At the next lesson, the teacher can add a sticker to the box.

- ❑ Participate in a sponsored practice for charity, eg a sponsored paper-chain – one link for every five repetitions of an assigned section.

Positive attitude

- ❑ Make your child want to do it correctly – challenge your child.

- ❑ Instill the belief that your child can do any particular task.

- ❑ Be positive! Children concentrate more in class when their teachers praise them than when they are criticised. As an experiment, try not using the word "No" in your child's practice for the next seven days. Does this make your child more relaxed and more co-operative?

- ❑ Always finish the practice with something special – a favourite piece or a concert piece.

Charts and other aids

Practice charts and stickers are useful as they give children a visible reminder of their achievements.

Practice sheets

- ❑ Make a list of all the pieces in your child's repertoire. Each time a piece is played, give it a tick, colour in a square or add a sticker (for pianists, sometimes ask for each hand separately and then hands together to qualify for a tick or sticker).

- ❑ Design an attractive chart to fill in, with a reward at the end if no days are missed, eg a concert, DVD or outing. Try ten consecutive days of practice, or fifty, or a hundred!

Pictures

- ❑ Colour part of a picture after every practice and show the teacher at the next lesson.

- ❑ Paint a picture to show progress in practice – a night sky and add stars for good practising, or a bus and draw people in the bus, or a bare tree and attach paper leaves.

- ❑ Draw a dragon. For every repetition of the teacher's assignment collect a piece of coloured paper. At the end of the practice stick the papers onto the dragon as his scales. This works well as a team effort for siblings all learning instruments as they urge each other on to earn more pieces of paper to finish a part of the dragon.

- ❑ Draw some islands and make movable ships that sail centimetre by centimetre towards the islands with each piece or repetition. Collect treasure (eg a raisin or chocolate button) when a ship reaches an island.

Stickers and stampers

❑ Buy a picture rubber stamp and ink block – stamp a picture for every piece played.

❑ Buy a book of picture stickers. After each good practice choose a sticker and add it to a chart displayed on the wall so as to make a story.

Lucky dip box

❑ Make lucky dip boxes – one box with slips of paper for each phrase of a piece, eg phrase 1 or 2 or 3 or 4; one box with 1x, 2x, 3x or 4x – then play that phrase that number of times.

❑ Have a lucky dip box to practise certain techniques – eg two bars from each of four different pieces for smooth bow changes, to improve awkward fingering, or for good echoes.

❑ Make a lucky dip with pieces of paper with the names of all your child's repertoire pieces – transfer the papers from one box to another as the pieces are played.

Chapter 13: Developing performance skills

Thorough preparation for performance will help you perform at your best. If you need an accompaniment, rehearse carefully with your accompanist. Listen to recordings of your piece(s) so you know how your part fits with the accompaniment and what goes on during any bars of silence in your part. Practise performing in different situations, including informally to family and friends, before playing for exams and auditions, in competitions, festivals and concerts.

Performance preparation

- ❑ Spend one week practising your piece *only* very slowly, then (pianists) one week practising it *only* hands separately.

- ❑ Practise with the metronome (pianists – hands separately, then together).

- ❑ Practise with your eyes closed – listening carefully.

- ❑ Listen to all the recordings you have of your piece. Analyse and compare the recordings, decide what you like about them and what you would like different. Play with the recordings, then play solo.

- ❑ If your solo requires piano or orchestral accompaniment, it is essential to familiarise yourself with the accompaniment. Do this by listening to professional recordings of your piece (sometimes miming or playing with the recording) and also rehearsing with your accompanist (if possible, do this prior to the day of the performance).

- ❑ Record yourself and listen back to your recording, assessing carefully what you like about it and what could be changed or improved.

- ❑ Play from the beginning of the piece; at every slip, missed note, smudge or poor sound – stop and practise that bar, put the bar into context by starting a few bars earlier, then go back to the beginning of the phrase or section and keep playing until the next slip.

- ❑ Challenge yourself to play it until it is right, which may be only once if you are really concentrating!

- ❑ Practise so your worst is good enough – nerves are caused partly by a lack of thorough preparation.

Performance practice

- ❑ At the end of each practice, play through your piece as if performing – ignoring slips, keeping going come what may. Concentrate on playing expressively – shaping the phrases musically.

- ❑ Go to your instrument two or three times a day during the week leading up to a performance (separate from your 'practice time') and perform your piece with no warm ups – straight through, no stops.

- ❑ Imagine playing to an audience – imagine how you would like to feel when performing.

❑ Practise performing informally in many different situations.

❑ Practise performing in unfamiliar surroundings – in different rooms and halls.

❑ Practise performing in your concert clothes, including shoes.

❑ Visualise your complete performance – rehearse mentally.

❑ Experience other performing art forms, including public speaking.

Performing

❑ At the beginning, look at your audience – smile – bow – look at your audience.

❑ Take your time getting ready with your instrument (eg if a pianist, adjust the height of the stool, sit down and rest your hands in your lap), hear the music in your head before starting to play.

❑ Overload your performance with musical ideas – have so much in your head to think about you have no time to be nervous.

❑ Relate to your audience – don't block them out.

❑ Enjoy sharing your love of music with your audience.

❑ Avoid turning your back to your audience when moving to take your bow.

❑ At the end, smile – bow – smile again – share your audience's pleasure.

Performance opportunities

Young children, up to the age of about 10 or 11, tend not to get unduly nervous about performing, especially if they know they are well prepared. During these early years, it is valuable for children to have as many good performing experiences as possible. As they approach their teens they become more self-conscious, and plenty of early positive experiences will set them up well for further performances.

.... created by parents

Parents may create performance opportunities for their children in the following ways:

❑ Arrange a weekly performance to both parents, or the whole family, either of your child's complete repertoire or of the latest 'perfect' piece; or a teddy bear concert attended by all your child's soft toys, all of whom require tickets!

❑ When relatives come to visit, arrange in advance with your children *what* they will perform, and *when* – perhaps immediately before or just after tea (and give them their favourite teatime treat).

❑ Invite two or three other musical families for an afternoon – each child plays one or two pieces, followed by a party to which each family contributes to the food.

❑ Ask at school whether your child may play to the class or at assembly; or at church or a local club.

Reward a performance with an outing, especially musical, or other celebration, so your child will have positive memories of the performing occasion.

.... *created by teachers*

Teachers may create regular performance opportunities at various levels:

- ❑ Ask students to 'perform' a piece to you in lesson, including bowing (and, if appropriate, announcing their piece) – a practice 'concert performance'.

- ❑ If you encourage observers to attend lessons, then already in lessons the pupil is 'performing' to a small audience.

- ❑ If you give group lessons in addition to individual lessons, or if your normal teaching is in a group, then pupils have a ready-made audience to whom they can perform prepared pieces, either solo or ensemble.

- ❑ Arrange regular informal concerts in your teaching studio.

- ❑ Organise formal concerts in hired halls.

- ❑ Combine your concerts with those of other teachers, including teachers of other instruments, for solo performances and/or ensemble items, eg some of your pupils could be accompanied by pupils of a piano teacher colleague.

- ❑ Participate in festivals and competitions.

- ❑ Take part in national performing opportunities, eg through national music associations.

Ensure concerts and other performing opportunities are followed by tea parties and social events so the whole performing experience is a really enjoyable one for everybody.

Chapter 14: Playing from memory

There are many advantages to memorising music. Knowing a piece really well allows you to concentrate on your own interpretation in performance, and an intense familiarity enhances your ability to communicate the music to the audience. Indeed, audiences prefer memorised performances. Playing from memory enables you to concentrate on the sound and to understand the whole composition more readily – the music transfers more fluently from conception to performance with no intermediate score. There is the added bonus of being able to give impromptu performances to family and friends.

There can be disadvantages of performing from memory. The ability to play from memory varies, and a nervous performer may break down completely with no music. Early errors in learning the score may become reinforced and a particular interpretation may become fixed. However, even if you do not attain the security to perform without the music, the exercise of memorising is highly beneficial in making you attend to the detail of the piece. The more you follow the music with your eyes, the less you may be attending to the sound.

People vary in their memorising preferences. Those with strong aural memory may like to play a piece and then listen back to it in their head. Those with strong visual memory will look at the music and then repeat short passages at their instrument. Kinaesthetic memory involves miming a piece, perhaps on a table top. Analytical memorisers will examine the piece for its structure.

Security of performing from memory comes from memorising in several different ways. Here are ten different approaches to memorising. Adopting as many methods as possible should lead to greater success.

Ten points for successful memorising

1 Start by memorising as soon as you begin to learn the piece
2 Analyse the structure of the piece
3 Focus on the musical patterns
4 Break down difficult passages
5 Rehearse in your mind without playing – mental rehearsal
6 Once piece is known – correct from memory not the music
7 Practise starting from anywhere in the piece
8 Play the piece frequently and regularly
9 Listen to master performances
10 The more you memorise, the easier it becomes

Start by memorising

After playing through the piece a couple of times to get the gist of it, memorising should begin immediately (rather than first learning a piece, and then deciding to commit it to memory). However, it is essential to return repeatedly to the score to ensure musical details and fingering are being learned correctly. Take note of repeats of material which are similar but different. At an early stage of studying the piece, select and practise certain features of the music to help remember the next section. Singers are advised to memorise by linking the words and the music, rather than learning the two separately.

Analyse structure

Pure repetition is an inefficient way of memorising. If music is memorised subconsciously, with no conscious effort, it can be retrieved only in the same way, and when the performer tries to think about the music rather than playing automatically, the memory fails. It is essential to support memory of the sounds, movements and sight with analysis of the structure of the music – understanding the harmonic changes, the melodic sequences, the rhythmic patterns and the form of the piece. In this way, material to be remembered is related to other relevant information. Try to develop a map of the piece in your mind by thinking about the structure of the music. Identify patterns, such as a phrase returning in a different key, inverted, or with a different rhythm, articulation or dynamic. Memorise harmonic structure rather than individual notes, as in reading "cat" not "C-A-T". This leads to music being permanently stored in the memory and immediately accessible.

See **Analysis of folk song: Go tell Aunt Rhody** below.

Go tell Aunt Rhody

Folk Song

Analysis of folk song: Go tell Aunt Rhody

When learning a new piece, it is useful to analyse its structure, eg to work out which parts repeat where. In this way you can work out what are the different sections to be practised. A piece that seems long may, in fact, have fewer notes to learn than you thought at first.

Check that, on repeats of similar sections, you always use the same fingering, articulation, bowing, breathing, dynamics, etc. Or, indeed, not – it may be appropriate to vary some of the musical elements on each repeat (though probably fingerings should remain constant). But you need to be clear in your mind what you want to do where.

Also, when memorising, it is important to be fully aware of the structure of the piece, otherwise it's very easy to take a wrong turning and either omit a section or find you're back at the beginning of the piece when you should be near the end.

Form
Aunt Rhody is a very simple example of a piece in ternary form. Ternary means it has three sections: A (bars 1-4), B (bars 5-8), and a repeat of A (bars 9-12), ie A B A.

Harmony
Looking at the left hand, each group of four notes comprises one chord. The first two chords are C major chords, the third is G major, the next C major. These four chords (C-C-G-C) repeat in the next two bars. Bar 5 again contains two C major chords, bar 6 starts with an F major chord followed by a C major chord. This pattern (C-C-F-C) repeats in the next two bars. Bars 9-12 repeat bars 1-4 exactly (except the last note is different to allow the piece to finish in bar 12).

Instead of playing the left hand as written (as broken chords), one could practise the left hand as block chords (playing the three notes of each chord simultaneously) to help learn the harmonic structure of the piece.

Rhythm
Look at the rhythm of the melody (right hand) in the first two bars and compare it with the rhythm of the next two bars. They are very similar. The rhythm of bar 3 is identical to that of bar 1. Bars 3+4 answer bars 1+2. Compare the rhythms of bars 1-4 with bars 5-8. The first three bars are identical; the fourth bar is slightly different. Bars 9-12 are identical with bars 1-4.

Melody
Compare the shape of the melody in bar 1 with that in bar 3. The shape is identical – bar 3 is written higher. Compare the shape of bar 1 with bar 5. Bar 1 starts with a repeated note, goes down and down again, and repeats that note. Bar 5 starts with a repeated note, goes up and up again, and repeats that note. Bars 2 and 6, likewise, are similar.

Focus on musical patterns

It is more important to concentrate on the *musical* aspects of a piece than the *technical* aspects when memorising. These aspects might include identifying phrase shapes, climaxes and the emotional colour of the music. Experienced performers are very flexible about solving minor memory problems. Novice performers should be able to give fine performances if they play music that is both musically and technically well within their grasp.

Break down difficult passages

Effective practice requires breaking down and repeating passages that are causing difficulty. To prevent errors, practising slowly and then gradually bringing the piece up to full speed is often required. Playing from memory very slowly will develop security. For pianists, practising hands separately prior to practising hands together results in greater security and clarity. It is strongly recommended to memorise each hand separately, especially the left hand. Particularly troublesome passages can be played slowly in different keys. Careful and consistent fingerings are essential when memorising.

Work by repeating short sections of the music. Beginners need to work with shorter sections, more advanced students with longer sections. The more difficult the music, the shorter the sections into which it will need to be divided. As the music becomes more familiar, sections for practice will become longer to reflect the musical value of thinking in larger units.

Rehearse mentally

Professional musicians are able to think through the music away from their instrument. They rehearse the music in their minds. They feel the dance or the song of the music, getting an overall view of the emotional landscape. Miming the music from memory at the instrument is another valuable method of developing security. Those who are more able to visualise the score and hear it with their 'inner ear' are quicker and more accurate in memorising the music. Mental rehearsal is important in conjunction with physical rehearsal. However, the less advanced the musician, and the more difficult the music, the more important motor practice becomes over mental rehearsal.

Correct from memory

If mistakes are made when practising from memory, it is important to listen and correct the errors by ear, rather than refer to the music, in order to develop aural awareness and security. Place the score nearby, where it can be referred to after finishing playing, rather than on the music stand where it may be glanced at during playing. Playing with the eyes shut helps develop a physical awareness of the required movements and enhances the ability to listen. However, it is also advisable regularly to play memorised pieces from the music in order to remind oneself of all the musical details written in the score.

Practise starting anywhere

A memory of the physical movements – kinaesthetic memory – will develop as a piece is practised repeatedly. One problem with kinaesthetic memorising is that if something does go wrong in performance, it may be very difficult to re-establish the musical thought and continue the performance. It is therefore important to identify strategic points in the music and practise starting from each of them. Also useful is to mime picking up from any bar in the music.

Play piece frequently

Practising a piece several times during the day offers repeated opportunities for the music to transfer from short-term to long-term memory. Music rehearsed for a short time twice a day will be better known and memorised at the end of a week than music played for a long time once during the week. In other words, regular, shorter practices are more beneficial than infrequent, long practices.

Listen to performances

Listen extensively to master performances of the music you are learning, as well as to other music by the same and contemporary composers. This makes playing from memory easier, for your 'inner ears' become well developed. When performing, the music continues in your head, whatever the fingers do. Odd slips of the fingers are not distracting because you have the larger picture – the musical structure – in your mind.

Memorise more

Practise performing to others in all sorts of situations in order to build confidence. The ability to memorise music may depend on how much you have already memorised, and the more you perform from memory, the easier it will become. One successful memorised performance increases confidence so the task becomes less demanding next time. Inexperienced memorisers should start by memorising an easy piece, progressively setting themselves longer and more challenging music to memorise.

Epilogue

Much enjoyment is to be had from playing music. Musicians continually seek an interpretation so their musical experiences are communicated to their audience. When performers feel in control of their technique, it is easier for them to give voice to their emotions, and their performances will give greater pleasure to themselves and their listeners.

Learning to play an instrument well requires an ability to question, to be curious, to be intrigued, to look outside the musical and technical issues at the broader view. I hope that, after studying this book, students will feel more able to question themselves on how they are working, challenge themselves to find more varied and interesting ways of practising and, thereby, make more progress in their ability to play skilfully and expressively.

Learning an instrument involves discovering how to tackle difficulties – through analysing the problem, devising a strategy to overcome it, and applying that strategy. It requires self-discipline to dedicate time to practise. Arguably, playing an instrument develops co-ordination, memory, and mental agility. It is possible that improvements in these areas will enhance self-esteem.

Above all, patience must be learned. The Zen master, Dogen, replied to a young monk who was anxious that his progress was slow:

The joyfully seeking mind is primary

Afterword: The Buddha at the keyboard

An epitome of mindful practice

The performer is the organism through which the music is realised. The music is not to be conceived as that through which the performer is revealed, but in realising the music the character of the performer will be expressed. If the self is forgotten, it appears at its best in the sound.

There are no short cuts. If an imperfection is overlooked in order to finish learning, the defect becomes entrenched. Catch a fault as early as possible. It cannot always be eradicated quickly, nor can a difficulty be overcome in a single session. A passage is not improved by mere repetition. The means whereby it is to be realised must be reconceived, and repeated experiment in reconception may be needed, sometimes over many sessions.

Cultivate economy. Be aware of movements, and remove any that are superfluous, including unnecessary muscular tension. Be aware of thoughts that wander, and bring attention back where it belongs. Pauses for assessment of economy and attention must be frequent.

Endurance is limited, and the principal constraint is on the power of attention. Frequent pauses should prevent physical fatigue, partly through the rest inherent in stopping, and partly through effects on the cultivation of economy. When it becomes impossible to overcome flagging attention, practice should cease until the mind is refreshed.

Do not be elated by success, nor downcast by failure. Do not curse wrong notes, nor agonise over failure to overcome problems. Such suffering results from the intrusion of ego, and hinders accomplishment. In the perfected state, the only consciousness is musical. Freedom is attained, and with it incomparable happiness, a glimpse of nirvana.

Jimmy Altham

Glossary

The following terms have been used in this book.

Italian terms

Italian term	Abbreviation	Meaning
subito piano	*sub p*	suddenly soft
pianissimo	*pp*	very soft
piano	*p*	soft
mezzo piano	*mp*	fairly soft
mezzo forte	*mf*	fairly strong
forte	*f*	strong
sforzando	*sf*	accented
diminuendo	*dim*	gradually getting softer
crescendo	*cresc*	gradually getting stronger
staccato	*stacc*	detached
legato	*leg*	smooth
non legato	*non leg*	not smooth – slightly detached
tenuto	*ten*	held
tempo		speed
vibrato		literally shaken, vibrating – a slight wavering of pitch, especially on stringed and wind instruments and voice, to enrich and intensify the tone
rubato		literally robbed, stolen – strict time is disregarded – what is robbed from some notes is paid back to others

Technical terms for notes of scale

Technical term	Meaning
tonic	first note of scale – key-note – home
dominant	fifth note of scale, so called because it is a very important note which dominates the key

Note values

Sign	British name	American name
♩	minim	half note
♩	crotchet	quarter note
♪	quaver	eighth note
♫	pair of quavers	pair of eighth notes
♪	semiquaver	sixteenth note
♫	dotted quaver-semiquaver	dotted eighth note-sixteenth note
𝄽	crotchet rest	quarter note rest
𝄾	quaver rest	eighth note rest

Musical forms

Form	Description
binary	a piece in two sections: A B
ternary	a piece in three sections – the first is repeated (possibly varied) after the second: A B A
rondo	a piece in which the first section is interspersed with contrasting episodes: A B A C A
sonata form	an extended piece – in the first section the themes are presented (exposed), in the second they are developed, and in the third they are repeated (recapitulated) but now staying nearer the tonic: exposition – development – recapitulation

Further reading and study

I have found few books on practising aimed at students or parents. Hence my desire to write *Successful Practising*. The books and DVD below have provided inspiration for my teaching.

Alcantara, P. de (1997) *Indirect Procedures: A Musician's Guide to the Alexander Technique*. New York, USA: Oxford University Press.

Anderson, S. (2006) *Keyboard Skills for Reluctant Pianists: A Do-It-Yourself Manual for Students*. London, UK: Marco Publications.

Berman, B. (2000) *Notes from the Pianist's Bench.* New Haven, USA and London UK: Yale University Press.

Coyle, D. (2010) *The Talent Code.* London, UK: Arrow Books, Random House.

Galamian, I. (1964) *Principles of Violin Playing and Teaching*. London, UK: Faber and Faber.

Gerle, R. (1983) *The Art of Practising the Violin*. London, UK: Stainer and Bell.

Harris, P.(2006) *Improve your teaching! An essential handbook for instrumental and singing teachers*. London, UK: Faber Music.

Harris, P.(2008) *Improve your teaching! Teaching Beginners A new approach for instrumental and singing teachers*. London, UK: Faber Music.

Harris, P, & Crozier, R. (2000) *The Music Teacher's Companion: A Practical Guide*. London, UK: The Associated Board of the Royal Schools of Music.

Hewitt, A. (2008) *Bach Performance on the Piano*. London, UK: Hyperion (DVD).

Mackworth-Young, L. (2000) *Tuning In: Practical Psychology for Musicians who are Teaching, Learning and Performing*. Swaffham, UK: MMM Publications.

McLachlan, M. (2006/07) The Practice List. *International Piano Magazine*, Part 1, IP48 November/December 2006 and Part 2, IP49 January/February 2007.

McTier, D. (1999) *Tips and Tricks, Volume 1: Preparation and Practise*. Twickenham, UK: McTier Music MM402.

Oglethorpe, S. (2001) *Instrumental Music for Dyslexics: A Teaching Handbook*. London, UK: Whurr Publishers.

Parncutt, R. & McPherson, G.E. (Eds.) (2002) *The Science and Psychology of Music Performance: Creative Strategies for Teaching and Learning*. New York, USA: Oxford University Press.

Ristad, E. (1982) *A Soprano on Her Head: Right-side-up reflections on life and other performances*. Moab, UT, USA: Real People Press.

Taylor, H. (1994) *The Pianist's Talent: A new approach to piano playing based on the principles of F Matthias Alexander and Raymond Thiberge*. London, UK: Kahn and Averill.

Taylor, K. (1993) *Principles of Piano Technique and Interpretation*. London and Sevenoaks, UK: Novello and Co.

Varro, M. (1997) *Dynamic Piano Teaching*. London, UK: N. Simrock.

Waterman, F, (2006) *On Piano Teaching and Performing*. London, UK: Faber Music.

Westney, W. (2003) *The Perfect Wrong Note: Learning to Trust your Musical Self*. Pompton Plains, NJ, USA: Amadeus Press.

References

1   McLachlan, M. (2006/07) The Practice List. *International Piano Magazine*, Part 1, IP48 November/December 2006 and Part 2, IP49 January/February 2007.

2   Harris, P. (2006) *Improve your teaching! An essential handbook for instrumental and singing teachers*. London, UK: Faber Music.

3   Ericsson, A., Krampe, R. & Tesch-Romer, C. (1993) The role of deliberate practice in the acquisition of expert performance. *Psychological Review*, 100: 363-406.

4   Coyle, D. (2010) *The Talent Code.* London, UK: Arrow Books, Random House.

5   Jean Hickson, unpublished article.

6   Hallam, S. (1998) *Instrumental Teaching – a practical guide to better teaching and learning.* Oxford, UK: Heinemann.

7   Ascribed to Julian Lloyd-Webber.

8   O'Connor, J. (1987/1997) *Not Pulling Strings.* London, UK: Lambent Books.

9   Shenk, D. (2002) *The Forgetting: Understanding Alzheimer's: A Biography of a Disease.* London, UK: HarperCollins.

10 Davidson, J.W., Howe, M.J.A., Moore, D.G. & Sloboda, J.A. (1996) The role of parental influences in the development of musical performance. *British Journal of Developmental Psychology*, 14: 399-412.

11 Hornby, G. (2000) *Improving parental involvement*. London, UK: Cassell.

12 National Literacy Trust (2001) *Parental involvement and literacy achievement: the research evidence and the way forward. A review of the literature*. www.literacytrust.org.uk.

13 Irish National Teachers' Organisation (1997) *Parental involvement: possibilities for partnership*. Dublin, Eire: INTO.

14 Cairney, T.H. & Munsie, L. (1992) *Beyond Tokenism: parents as partners in literacy*. Victoria, Australia: Australian Reading Assocation.

15 Macmillan, J. (2003) *Learning the Piano: Teachers' attitudes to parental involvement*. Unpublished MA dissertation, University of Sheffield, UK.

16 Sloboda, J.A. (1993) Becoming a Musician. Paper presented at the Annual Meeting of the *British Association for the Advancement of Science*. University of Keele, UK.

17 Pitts, S.E., Davidson. J.W. & McPherson, G.E. (2000) Developing effective practice strategies: Case studies of three young instrumentalists. *Music Education Research*, 2/1: 45-56.

18 Lehmann, A.C. & Ericsson, K.A. (1997) Research on expert performance and deliberate practice: implications for the education of amateur musicians and music students. *Psychomusicology*, 16/1: 40-58.

19 du Pré, H. & P. (1998) *A Genius in the Family*. London, UK: Vintage: 29-30.

20 Turner, A. (1992) The Whole Child. *Music Teacher*, January 1992.

21 da Costa, D. (1999) An investigation into instrumental pupils' attitudes to varied, structured practice. *British Journal of Music Education*, 16/1: 65-77.

22   Clemson, G. (1998) Ten tips for carefree cello practice, *Ability Development*, Autumn 1998.

23   Barry, N.H. & Hallam, S. (2002) Practice. In R. Parncutt & G.E. McPherson (Eds.) *The Science and Psychology of Music Performance*. New York, USA: Oxford University Press, 151-165.

24   Coyle, D. (2010) *The Talent Code.* London, UK: Arrow Books, Random House.

25   Westney, W. (2003) *The Perfect Wrong Note: Learning to Trust your Musical Self*. Pompton Plains, NJ, USA: Amadeus Press.

26   Roskell, P. (2004) *Yoga for Musicians*. 66 Queen Elizabeth's Walk, London, N16 5UQ, UK, peneloperoskell@yahoo.co.uk.

27   Ascribed to Heinrich Neuhaus.

28   McTier, D. (1999) *Tips and Tricks, Volume 1: Preparation and Practice*. Twickenham, UK: McTier Music MM402.

29   Hewitt, A. (2008) *Bach Performance on the Piano*. London, UK: Hyperion (DVD).

30   Williamon, A. (2004) *Musical Excellence: Strategies and techniques to enhance performance*. New York, USA: Oxford University Press.

31   Hofnote. www.hofnote.com.

32   Computer Aided Theory Skills. www.takenotepublishing.co.uk/tnpl/cats.

Index